SHAMBHALA DRAGON EDITIONS

The dragon is an age-old symbol of the highest spiritual essence, embodying wisdom, strength, and the divine power of transformation. In this spirit, Shambhala Dragon Editions offers a treasury of readings in the sacred knowledge of Asia. In presenting the works of authors both ancient and modern, we seek to make these teachings accessible to lovers of wisdom everywhere.

Books by Traleg Kyabgon

The Essence of Buddhism
Mind at Ease
The Practice of Lojong

THE
ESSENCE of
BUDDHISM

An Introduction to
Its Philosophy and Practice

TRALEG KYABGON

SHAMBHALA
Boston & London
2001

Shambhala Publications, Inc.
Horticultural Hall
300 Massachusetts Avenue
Boston, Massachusetts 02115
www.shambhala.com

18 17 16 15 14 13 12 11 10

Printed in the United States of America

⊗ This edition is printed on acid-free paper that meets the
American National Standards Institute z39.48 standard.
♻ This book is printed on 30% postconsumer recycled paper.
For more information please visit www.shambhala.com.
Distributed in the United States by Random House, Inc.
and in Canada by Random House of Canada Ltd.

LIBRARY OF CONGRESS CATALOGING-IN-PUBLICATION DATA
Kyabgon, Traleg, 1955–
The essence of Buddhism: an introduction to its philosophy and
practice / by Traleg Kyabon.
p. cm.—(Shambhala dragon editions)
ISBN 978-1-57062-468-1 (pbk.)
1. Religious life—Buddhism. 2. Buddhism—Doctrines.
I. Title
BQ4302 K93 2000
294.3'4—dc21
99-089434

This book is dedicated to
His Holiness the Dalai Lama,
His Holiness the sixteenth Karmapa,
and His Eminence Drugpa Thugsey Rinpoche.

CONTENTS

Contents

PREFACE

It might seem that there is no need for another introductory book on Buddhism, since today there is a plethora of quality books available on the market, which was not the case a decade ago. However, after some thought, I was persuaded that there may be room for another book, one that introduces the general public to the Tibetan form of Buddhism approached from the perspective of the Kagyü school, which is the second oldest lineage of Tibetan Buddhism. It seems to me that some introductory books are either too elementary or too scholarly to be immediately accessible to newcomers to Buddhism. Moreover, I have not yet seen an accessible introductory book that makes the teachings on the three yanas of Tibetan Buddhism easily understandable to a student who is totally new to Buddhism or even to more experienced students. As a writer, one has a dilemma over how much detail to present. I have tried to maintain this difficult balance so that the text will be neither too shallow nor too dense and inaccessible.

The text—based upon teachings I have given in Australia, Europe, and the United States—is divided into three parts, each devoted to one of the three yanas. Chapters 1 through 4 introduce the student to the basic principles of early Buddhist teachings. Here the teachings on the Four Noble Truths and Buddhist training on moral precepts, concentration, and wisdom are discussed in some detail. The fourth chapter is devoted to karma and rebirth, which is a central feature in traditional Tibetan Buddhist teachings.

The second part is devoted to sutric Mahayana teachings and tantric Mahayana teachings. Here I deal with what sort of obstacles, impediments, and obscurations we need to overcome, the means we employ to overcome them, and the result of having used these antidotes. This is presented from the point of view of the sutric and tantric descriptions of the path and stages of spiritual development.

The final part is devoted to the teachings and to meditation, which is seen as the culmination of the three-yana system, and that is from the point of view of the Mahamudra tradition, which is seen as going beyond Tantra itself.

It is my wish that this book will be of use to newcomers and to seasoned Buddhists as well. In my mind, if only one person is turned toward the Dharma for having read this book, I will feel more than amply rewarded.

ACKNOWLEDGMENTS

I WOULD LIKE TO THANK all of my students to whom I have had the opportunity to give discourses and discuss the topics broached in this book. I have always found teaching to be the best way to learn the Dharma. Teaching the Buddha-Dharma is just as beneficial and profitable as is receiving the teachings from a living master. Everything I know about Buddhism I learned from Khenpo Sodar and Khenpo Noryang of Sangngag Choling Monastery in Darjeeling, India. I would like to thank Deirdre Collings and Vyvyan Cayley for their help in preparing this book. I would also like to thank Samuel Bercholz for his inspiration and encouragement and Kendra Crossen Burroughs for her excellent editorial work. And I would like to thank Shambhala Publications for allowing this book to see the light of day.

The Essence of Buddhism

I

FUNDAMENTALS

The Four Noble Truths and the Eightfold Noble Path

IN THIS BOOK we shall look at various aspects of the Buddhist tradition, and in particular at how Buddhism developed as a philosophy. This is so that we can get a comprehensive idea of Buddhism as a whole, because the type of Buddhism practiced by Tibetans is not based on one particular school of Buddhism as such; rather, it tries to incorporate a variety of practices and philosophical thought from many different traditions. This is known as the "three *yanas*" perspective on Buddhism. *Yana* (Sanskrit) is the spiritual "vehicle" that transports the individual from the samsaric condition to the freedom of nirvana.

So even though Tibetan Buddhists may emphasize certain aspects of Mahayana teachings, this does not mean that they do not practice any aspect of the Theravadin tradition as we find it in Thailand, Sri Lanka, and other countries. Some people feel that Tibetan Buddhism has no link or association with the Buddhism that is practiced in those countries. But Tibetan Buddhism contains elements of teachings as we find them in all parts of the world—for example, we can even find elements of the Zen tradition in Tibetan Buddhism.

The Buddha's Awakening

Buddhism was founded by the Buddha about twenty-five hundred years ago. What we know about the Buddha is that he claimed to have seen the reality of things and to have gained enormous insight into the nature of the human condition. He did not claim to be an incarnation of some higher being nor to be a messenger of any kind. Neither did he say that he was an intermediary between some higher reality and human beings. He said that he was an ordinary human being who applied himself through the practice of meditation and was able to purify his own mind, so that insight was born in him, enabling him to see things as they are. And Buddha also said that this ability can be developed by anyone.

At the time of the Buddha, some people were claiming that only those of a certain social standing who were sanctioned by a divine being had the ability to aspire toward higher religious goals, while other, "lesser" beings did not have that ability. Others were saying that men had the ability to develop themselves spiritually but women lacked that capacity. The Buddha said that this ability to develop in a religious sense has nothing to do with our social or cultural background, our religious background, or even our sex, but is available to everyone who spends the time and makes the effort to develop the insight. For this reason Buddha is known as the Enlightened One, because to gain this insight into the nature of things is to become enlightened, and that is the same as Buddhahood. The word *buddha* literally means "awakened."

As ordinary human beings we are not fully awake, because our thoughts and behavior are conditioned by ignorance, confusion, misunderstanding, and lack of insight. When the mind is purified of all these defilements or pollutants (also referred to as "obscurations") and the consciousness becomes pure and aware, then one is able to realize the nature of things; and this is the same as the attainment of Buddhahood.

We must remember that the Buddha gave these teachings within the context of the Indian tradition. He rejected two major Indian traditions. One is the teachings that came from the Upanishads, which emphasized the importance of realizing the nature of one's own self as being identical with the reality of the world. The essence of the world is perceived as Brahman, the Absolute, and this is identical with the pure nature of one's own self, which is Atman. Thus, the aim of a religious practitioner is to realize the identity of one's own higher self and the reality of the world. The Buddha rejected that as being an extreme position, which he called the eternalist or absolutist position.

He also rejected another extreme position, which was materialist-based. Believers in this extreme, called Ajivikas or Lokayatas, rejected the existence of consciousness and moral responsibility because they believed that we are made up of five elements that dissolve at the time of death, leaving nothing. There is no consciousness that persists after death, and because there is no consciousness we cannot talk of morality or anything of this nature, since these are just social conventions. The Buddha called these people nihilists.

He said that the followers of the Upanishads, the absolutists, overestimated reality, positing the existence of many kinds of things that in fact have no existence. The Buddha said that there is no essence or reality to be found either in the world or in the nature of the self; these are metaphysical constructions, fictions created by the human mind but not available to human experience.

At the same time, the nihilists underestimated reality by rejecting the existence of consciousness and so on. So the Buddha taught what he called the middle view. In terms of practice it is known as the Middle Way. The Buddha realized that many people either were very lax in their morality, overindulging in sense gratification, or engaged in extreme ascetic practices like self-mortification. According to the Buddha, both of these two methods are inappropriate for realizing the nature of reality. He himself engaged in ascetic practices for some time but found them wanting. However, he emphasized the importance of restraint and moderation, not falling into the extreme of overindulgence.

THE FOUR NOBLE TRUTHS
The Truth of Suffering

This teaching is contained in the Four Noble Truths, in which Buddha emphasized how the middle view is to be cultivated and how to practice the Middle Way. The first of the Four Noble Truths is suffering, which is the usual translation of the Sanskrit word *duhkha* (Pali, *dukkha*). We should qualify that translation by saying that this does not mean that the Buddha didn't acknowledge the existence of happiness or contentment in life. The point that he was making is that there is happiness and also sorrow in the world; but the reason why everything we experience in our everyday life is said to be duhkha is that even when we have some kind of happiness, it is not permanent; it is subject to change. So unless we can gain insight into that truth and understand what is really able to give us happiness, and what is unable to provide happiness, the experience of dissatisfaction will persist.

Normally we think our happiness is contingent upon external circumstances and situations, rather than upon our own inner attitude toward things, or toward life in general. The Buddha was saying that dissatisfaction is part of life, even if we are seeking happiness and even if we manage to find temporary happiness. The very fact that it is temporary means that sooner or later the happiness is going to pass. So the Buddha said that unless we understand this and see how pervasive dissatisfaction or *duhkha* is, it is impossible for us to start looking for real happiness.

According to the Buddha, even when we think we are trying to find real happiness, we are not doing it effectively, because we don't have the right attitude and we don't know where to look for it. The Buddha was not against happiness; rather, he gave us a method of finding out how to overcome that sense of dissatisfaction, and this method is part of the last Noble Truth. We shall come to that in a few pages.

The key to understanding the truth of suffering is what the Buddha called the "three marks" of everything that exists. All conditioned phenomena,* he said, are pervaded by these three marks: impermanence (*anitya*), dissatisfaction or suffering (*duhkha*), and insubstantiality (*anatman*, "without self"). According to the Buddha, if

---

*"Conditioned phenomena" (Skt. *samskrita;* Pali *sankhate*) means that everything that exists is mutually conditioned owing to causes and conditions: things come into existence, persist for some time, and then disintegrate, thus suggesting the impermanent nature of the empirical world.

we do not understand how conditioned phenomena are marked by these three aspects, then we will not be able to understand the first Noble Truth. We may do all we can in order to avoid facing the fact that everything is contingent and transient—we may try to hide ourselves from it, and we may even spin out all kinds of metaphysical theories of an unchanging, permanent, substantial reality to avoid this all-pervasive nature of ephemerality. Also, if we do not understand that conditioned phenomena are unsatisfactory, we will not think about restraining ourselves from overindulgence in sensory gratifications, which makes us lose our center and become immersed in worldly concerns, so that our life is governed by greed, craving, and attachment. All of these things disturb the mind. If we do not understand that everything is insubstantial—anatman—then we may believe that there is some kind of enduring essence or substance in things, or in the personality, and because of this belief we generate delusion and confusion in the mind.

The Origin of Suffering

The second Noble Truth is the origin of suffering, which means that once we have realized that suffering or dissatisfaction exist, we next have to find out where that suffering comes from: does it originate within, or does it come from some kind of external situation or condition? The Buddha said that when we start to examine ourselves and see how we respond to situations, how we act in the world, how we feel about things, then we will realize that the cause of suffering is within. This is not to say that external social or economic conditions don't create suffering; but the main suffering that afflicts us is created by our own mind and attitude.

The Buddha said that if we want to overcome dissatisfaction, which is intimately linked with our experience of suffering, then we have to deal with craving, grasping, clinging, and attachment—all these exaggerated forms of desire. Now, some people think that Buddhists encourage the idea of eradicating desire altogether, but that is not what the Buddha said. He said that we should try to overcome excessive and exaggerated forms of desire, which manifest as craving, grasping, and so on, because they make our condition worse by increasing our sense of dissatisfaction and discontentment. It is the more obsessive types of desire that the Buddha said we should try to overcome. As long as we have these strong forms of desire, they will always be accompanied by aversion, hatred, resentment, and so forth, because when we can't get what we want, we become frustrated, angry, and resentful. Or, if we find some obstacles in the way of satisfying our desire, we want to eliminate them, eradicate them, or attack them. We may even resort to violence and deception in order to satisfy our greed and craving. So the Buddha said that we need to deal with these extreme forms of desires; but we should not aim to eradicate desire altogether, because we can use desire in all kinds of positive ways as well. (We will look at that later.)

The Goal: The Cessation of Suffering

The third Noble Truth is the goal. First we find out about the human condition, how it is pervaded by a sense of dissatisfaction, then we look at the cause of that dissatisfaction, and after that we look at the goal, which is the attainment of *nirvana*. Some people think nirvana is some kind of absolute reality that is transcendent and otherworldly. But the Buddha said that one can attain nirvana while still living in this world; this is called "nirvana with remainder." One can also attain nirvana at the time of death, which is called "nirvana without remainder." So it is possible to achieve nirvana in this very lifetime. Achieving nirvana means that one's mind is no longer afflicted by delusion and emotional afflictions. The mind becomes tranquil, and one's experience of happiness is no longer dependent upon external situations and circumstances. Therefore, one's reaction to things is less extreme, and one is able to maintain a sense of tranquillity and peace, even when faced by adverse circumstances.

This is so because the one who has attained nirvana has overcome the three root delusions of attraction, aversion, and ignorance. When the mind is no longer governed by strong emotional reactions of either attraction and aversion, we can be at peace and tranquil even when things are not going right. We maintain a sense of fortitude and face things courageously.

The Path: The Way Out of Suffering

Having realized that this is the goal—to achieve a permanent happiness that is not based upon external changing conditions—we then have to find out how to apply ourselves in order to achieve that goal. This is what the fourth Noble Truth explains. The fourth Noble Truth is the path, and this is the essence of Buddhist practice. Known as the Eightfold Noble Path, it is oriented toward developing three things in an individual: moral sensitivity, meditation or the concentrated mind, and wisdom. Through the practice of moral sensitivity we become better individuals, able to overcome our egocentric tendencies. We become more compassionate and more sensitive to the needs of others. Through the practice of meditation our mind becomes more focused, more resilient, and more aware, which in turn gives rise to wisdom.

The Eightfold Noble Path consists of Right Understanding, Right Thought, Right Speech, Right Action, Right Livelihood, Right Effort, Right Mindfulness, and Right Concentration. The first two truths of Right Understanding and Right Thought correspond to the development of wisdom. Right Speech, Right Action, and Right Livelihood all develop our moral sensitivities. The last three—Right Effort, Right Mindfulness and Right Concentration—foster our meditative capabilities.

Right Understanding means understanding the Buddhist view, which, as we saw, is the middle view between eternalism and nihilism. As the Buddha said, knowing how the world arises due to causes and conditions enables us not to fall into the extreme of nihilism. The other aspect of the middle view is knowing how everything ceases when causes and conditions cease. Therefore, we do not fall into the extreme of the substantialist, essentialist, or eternalist view, because we realize that, even though things come into being through causes and conditions, nothing that exists on the physical or mental plane endures when those causes and conditions are no longer present.

Right Thought is associated with seeing how our thoughts and emotions are closely linked, and how indulging in negative forms of thought leads to the development of negative emotions such as hatred and jealousy. Conversely, thinking in a positive way has an effect on our emotions, whereby we start to become more loving, more caring, and more sensitive to others.

Right Speech means that if we are not aware—as normally we are not—then we don't know what we are saying or doing. Inadvertently, we indulge in all kinds of negative forms of speech such as lying, backbiting, haughty speech, and gossip. It is important to become aware of our speech, because what we say and how we say it have a direct influence on the kind of person we become. If we are always using harsh words, then we naturally become very aggressive.

Right Action relates to seeing how what we do is beneficial or harmful to ourselves and others. This is involved with developing *skill* in the way we act in the world. Instead of thinking that we already know what is the right thing to do and what is the wrong thing to do, in a clear-cut manner, it is important to look closely at the way we act. We should not simply rely on some preestablished rules or social norms; instead we should see how we as individuals act in the world and what the effects of our actions are upon ourselves, the environment, and other people.

With respect to Right Livelihood, the Buddha said that there is nothing wrong with making money and looking after one's family, but we must know how to make a living in a way that does not cause harm to others or ourselves. So, for example, we do not engage in an occupation that involves cruelty to animals or human beings, or one that obliges us to use deception or inflict physical or mental pain on others. If these things are involved, then we should give up that form of livelihood.

Right Effort has four aspects. The first effort has to do with prevention: making an effort through meditation to ensure that one does not yield to unwholesome thoughts and emotions, and trying to prevent these from arising in the mind. Unwholesome thoughts originate in attachment, aversion, and ignorance. The second effort is to reduce the unwholesome thoughts and emotions that have already arisen in the mind. The third effort is to develop wholesome thoughts and emotions, and this also is done in meditation. Even if they are not yet present, we should make an effort to arouse them. The fourth effort is to cultivate further those wholesome thoughts and emotions that have already risen in the mind.

Right Mindfulness is associated with becoming more attentive to our thoughts, emotions, feelings, speech, and behavior in meditation. Whatever we experience, we become more conscious of it and more attentive to it, so that we gain more insight into the workings of the mind and how the mind influences our actions in everyday life.

Right Concentration also develops from meditation. The mind becomes more focused and less distracted. Even if we hear or see or think of something, the mind does not become distracted but is still able to maintain a state of concentration.

So that is the Eightfold Noble Path, which leads the individual from this condition of *samsara** to the attainment of *nirvana*, or enlightenment. As we can see, the Four Noble Truths are both descriptive and prescriptive. They describe the condition we are in—what sort of conditions are prevalent and what the problems are. They also prescribe in terms of how to improve our situation, overcome our sense of dissatisfaction, and attain enlightenment through following the Eightfold Noble Path and its training in morality, meditation, and wisdom.

As I have said, the Four Noble Truths are the essence of all of the Buddha's teachings. Without understanding them, we cannot proceed. All the later interpretations of the original Buddhist teachings are based on the understanding of the Four Noble Truths. There may be different ways of understanding how we can train in meditation, wisdom, or morality, but there is no disagreement in terms of the importance of the understanding of the Four Noble Truths. All other practices are based upon or elaborate these fundamental teachings of Buddhism.

---

*Samsara (Skt.) is cyclic existence, in which—owing to the corrupting influences of the mental delusions of hatred, desire, and ignorance—sentient creatures are compelled to wander from one life form to another without respite until they meet up with the spiritual path.

2

ETHICAL CONDUCT

Doing What Is Truly Beneficial

FROM THE BUDDHIST POINT OF VIEW, a spiritual practitioner's ultimate aim is to attain self-realization or self-knowledge, to reach his
or her full potential. That is equated with Buddhahood or enlightenment. So for a Buddhist it is very important to understand the immediate condition that we are in and the experiences we have. When we
look around, we see that beings experience a lot of suffering in a
variety of ways.

We don't have to look very far to find suffering. Every time we
turn on the television we see suffering: in the Middle East, in Asia
and in Africa, in America. Suffering is endemic to the human condition. But when we talk about suffering in Buddhist terms, we don't
simply mean the suffering with which we can actually identify and
which we can label as real suffering. This kind of suffering is obvious, such as atrocities and oppression, repressive regimes that torture
innocent people, and so on.

When Buddhists talk about suffering, they mean other kinds of
suffering as well—experiences that we think are not suffering at all

but happiness, the ultimate goal that we should be striving toward. When we speak of *duhkha*, we mean a sense of dissatisfaction, which covers a whole range of human experiences.

THREE KINDS OF SUFFERING

From the Buddhist point of view, suffering can be experienced on three different levels. First is the suffering of pain (*duhkha-duhkhata*). This is the kind of obvious suffering of war, famine, political oppression, injustice, and so on.

Then there is the suffering of change (*viparinama-duhkhata*). That's the kind of suffering that we do not usually think of as real suffering. You may think, "Well, at work lately I've been under a lot of stress, but I'll take a holiday and have a good time, and then I'll be really happy." Then you go, and you may end up arguing with your partner or you may have a lot of problems with booking airfares; or when you arrive, your luggage may be lost and you can't recover it. You may have all kinds of experiences that you could not foresee, so that what is initially pleasurable can turn into a form of suffering. That's the suffering of change.

The last form of suffering is known as the suffering of conditioned existence (*samsara-duhkhata*), which means that just by virtue of being human or a living creature, we are a product of causes and conditions. When we are born, we experience birth trauma; when we grow up, we have all kinds of problems associated with adolescence; after that, we have problems associated with adulthood and finally with old age, with the weakening of the body. So we experience suffering, pain, and illness, and eventually we die and that's the end of the story. That is the human condition, that is what we have to deal with.

Some Western commentators on Buddhism have said that Buddhism is pessimistic because it concentrates so much on suffering. But actually, it is not pessimistic; it is realistic. The truth of suffering need not make us feel pessimistic and hopeless. There is a way that we can try to understand it. We have to be able to face up to unpleasant experiences and situations, the reality of things, the facts as they are.

That is the real concern of Buddhism; because if we are not able to do that, then we will have this temptation to think that what is not really the source of happiness is the one thing that is going to give us happiness. (I am going to explain what that means shortly.)

So first of all, when we understand that there is suffering in the world, we must correctly identify the source of that suffering. Suffering comes from within, from the mind. This is extremely important, because all kinds of people have tried to understand what is really the cause of suffering. Some people say that it is due to our sin, others say that it is because we have become distant from God or we have disobeyed God. Still others say it has to do with our social structures, our economic system, the repression of sexual instincts, childhood traumas, or alienation.

From the Buddhist point of view, these are just intermediary causes of our suffering rather than the real cause, which is ignorance: not knowing what is beneficial and what is not beneficial; not knowing what will really produce our happiness and what will increase our unhappiness and suffering. Lack of knowledge, lack of insight—this is the real cause.

So we have to look within. That does not mean we should disregard the injustice and repression that goes on in the world, but we should always look at these things as reflections of ourselves and what is going on in our own minds. What happens in the external world mirrors what is going on in the minds of individual human beings. We may blame a big corporation for being greedy, for exploiting a Third World country, and so on, but that may not be very different from small-business people doing exactly the same thing with their employees.

In Third World countries, people may look at the so-called First World countries with a sense of envy or hostility, and even with some kind of respect, a mixture of feelings. Similarly, we may look at people who are successful, who are millionaires, and feel a sense of envy, and also feel a sense of respect for the fact that they have achieved something we haven't. It is very easy to project all these things onto others and think that what is wrong is that society is not functioning well or that the big corporations are doing terrible things. In this way of thinking there is always someone else to blame, without looking at how the situation has come about in the first place.

Societies and big corporations are not amorphous entities but are made up of a collection of individuals just like ourselves. So for Buddhists it is not God who has created the world but our own mind— the mind is the one responsible for all our experiences: joy, happiness, pain, suffering. This is not only in terms of what we experience; the mind also fabricates the kind of world that we live in. The world that we live in is created by our mind.

Therefore, it is very important as a Buddhist to understand how the mind functions, and that is why the practice of meditation is so important for Buddhists. It has nothing to do with creating a state closer to a greater reality or some kind of spiritual reality that is independent of our mind. The practice of meditation has to do with the greater understanding of ourselves. A lot of our problems come about precisely because we do not understand ourselves, we do not have self-knowledge, we have no insight into ourselves. It is because of ignorance, which is called *avidya* in Sanskrit. In order to find out how the mind works, we have to see what sort of things will promote our happiness and what sort of things will increase our pain and suffering.

THE SEARCH FOR HAPPINESS

Normally we think that doing this, that, and the other thing will bring us happiness. We think, "When I get acknowledged by my friends, if they like me, then I'll be happy; if I'm married and have children and have a loving partner who will take care of me, then I'll be so happy; if I don't have to work so hard but have a lot of money, then I'll be so happy."

This line of thought is endless. If you are short, then you think that if you were tall you would be so happy; or if you were thin, then you'd be so happy. If you have a long nose, you think a smaller nose would be so wonderful; or if you are bald, you think you should have hair. Such beliefs do have an element of truth in them. Buddhists would agree that if you were healthier, of course you would be happier. If you had a supportive family, you would be much happier.

But the problem is that these things only produce temporary happiness, not lasting happiness. As Buddhists, our aim should not be just to achieve temporary happiness. Buddhists do not say that there is no happiness at all, or that no matter what you do it is all suffering, suffering, and more suffering. But we should have a proper perspective on our life, by which I mean that we should try to attain lasting happiness.

When we rely on temporary happiness, we are investing too much in something that is full of uncertainties. If we rely too much on our work, we may spend twenty years working for a particular company, and we put so much into it so that our whole perception of ourselves is fashioned by the work we do for that company and the kind of acquisitions we are able to realize as a result of that work. Then one day we may get sacked, and all of a sudden our whole reality falls apart and we feel like committing suicide. This actually happens to some people.

Buddhism says that we should have our own priorities in order. To obtain happiness, we must have inner peace. Real, lasting happiness is not obtained from an external source. This doesn't mean that we can't have happiness based upon external circumstances and situations, but the real, lasting happiness must come from within. When we become too dependent on external circumstances and situations, we lose ourselves in them. Instead of consolidating our identity, instead of finding ourselves, we actually lose ourselves. We all know this. We know a person who has been in a work environment for many, many years and who all of a sudden thinks, "Wait a minute, what have I been doing? I haven't done anything with my life." Or people who have been raising children for twenty or thirty years, always doing things for the family, for the kids. All of a sudden the mother might say, "Oh, look, I haven't done anything to find out who I am, what it is to be me." We can become completely lost, instead of finding ourselves. Normally our identity is almost exclusively conditioned by the kind of credentials we have, which school we went to, what sort of education we have had, what degrees we have, what sort of family we have, what suburb we live in, what car we drive. Buddhism says we should not rely too much on these things, because the car could be repossessed, or the liquidators could come and take our business away. Anything can happen. Your spouse may take on a lover, who knows? Of course, we should certainly aspire toward excellence in our work and parenting and so on, but we should keep things in perspective and not expect more than they can deliver.

Having realized that, we can move on to considering the Buddhist path as a means of overcoming this problem. As we have seen, the Eightfold Noble Path consists of training in morality (*shila*), meditation (*samadhi*), and wisdom (*prajna*). These three trainings basically enable us to change our behavior as well as our way of thinking and experiencing. Let us begin by concentrating on training in morality, or *shila*.

TRAINING IN MORALITY (*Shila*)

When we talk about morality, we normally think in terms of duty or obligation, but Buddhist morality is essentially concerned with what is beneficial (*kusala*) versus what is harmful (*akusala*). We should judge our actions in relation to whether we are benefiting ourselves and others or harming ourselves and others. In this way Buddhist morality is grounded in human experience. It has no reference to a supernatural being. We do not have to have a concept of a deity or God in order to have a concept of morality or to appreciate the importance of morality.

Some people feel that if we did not believe in God, then everything would be permissible; but then, on the other hand, those same people say that God has his own law, distinct from human law. The law or morality pertaining to human beings has no relevance when it comes to what God wants to do, in which case this human law and morality become arbitrary. This philosophical debate dates back to Plato, who asked: Is something good because God said it is good, or is it good independently of God? If it is good independently of God, then it has nothing to do with God; but if it is good only because God said so, then this means it is totally arbitrary.

According to Buddhism, a particular action is good because it is good in itself, not because God decreed it to be so. My point here is that Buddhist morality is not founded upon any theological basis whatsoever. What is a good action or what is a bad action is determined by a moral criterion only, not a theological one, and there is no need for theological justifications.

For Buddhists, a particular action is morally wrong precisely because it causes suffering to other people or to a large number of sentient beings. Thus, leading a moral life is not like being an obedient person or conforming to a preestablished law or norm. The Buddha said that morality should be seen as a liberating experience. Instead of being a constricting force that demands, "Thou shalt do this" or "Thou shalt not do that," morality is a liberating influence, because it can enhance our well-being.

Freud, who was brought up in the Jewish tradition, thought that the conflict between id and superego meant that the id wants to do nasty things and the superego says, "No, you can't." We are not thinking like this; instead of creating more conflict between what we want to do and what we are allowed to do, we find that what we *should* do will become what we *want* to do.

The Buddha said that shila is like a cool breeze that blows at midday or in the afternoon of an Indian summer. That cool breeze can be so refreshing. He said that when we start to practice morality in this way, we realize that all our mental agitation, all our resentment, hostility, and bitterness, actually begin to subside. Instead of increasing our mental agitation by thinking, "I'm on the side of the good and you're on the side of the evil, so let's fight," we begin to become more open and more understanding of people from different cultures and backgrounds. When we look at life not in terms of what is right and what is wrong, but in terms of what is beneficial and what is not beneficial, then we can have a different experience of morality.

It is a very important point, also, that doing what is "right" is not always beneficial, and doing what is "wrong" is not always harmful. Buddhist morality is not a self-imposed moral world unto itself. It is an open-ended one, and we have to use our own judgment much of the time, in terms of what is beneficial and what is harmful. Lacking in wisdom as we are, it is very difficult to foresee the consequences of our actions. But the other component of morality is motivation. If we do something with a pure intention, then even though, out of a lack of wisdom, our action may turn out harmful rather than beneficial, that action is not morally condemnable.

With this background of Buddhist ethics in mind, we can now look at the moral guidelines Buddha provided for his followers. Which actions should we refrain from and which actions should we take, with the view to helping ourselves and others?

Six Transcendental Actions (*Paramitas*)

First we look at what the Buddha thought we should strive toward. These actions are called *paramitas* (Tibetan, *pharol tu chimpa*), or "transcendental actions." The six paramitas are best known in Mahayana Buddhism, and I will return to these later. However, early Buddhism also talked about six paramitas. These transcendental actions are not oriented toward increasing our defilements or obscurations, or toward increasing our emotional conflict or conceptual confusions; they are actions that help to alleviate these very things.

The first one is giving. Apart from giving material things to the needy, it also involves social work and giving to relief funds and other charities. In Buddhist countries we also try to liberate captive animals, releasing fish into the sea or buying captive birds from the market and setting them free, as a way of giving back their life. This is seen as a very important practice. The effects of giving are important not only to the recipient but to the giver as well. When we learn to give, we become less attached and less dependent on our possessions. This is how we can learn to be less greedy and grasping.

The second practice is conduct. Conduct means that we take responsibility for our own actions. As soon as something goes wrong, instead of thinking that we are the victim of circumstances or of society or family upbringing, we should take full responsibility for our actions. In fact, when we take full responsibility for our actions, we become a full person and we begin to feel free, because freedom and responsibility go together. When we feel like the victim, there is no freedom; we feel impotent, incapacitated. But when we feel that we are responsible for our actions, then we feel free, because how can we be responsible for something if we have no choice?

The third paramita is restraint. This means that we should not be excessive in our indulgences or in our pursuit of pleasure. We should be aware of ourselves, so that we do not become addicted to whatever it is that gives us pleasure, and we should be able to make distinctions between our needs and our wants. We should not just go shopping for the sake of shopping, buying all those clothes that we will never wear or buying all kinds of gadgets that we will never use, and ending up being in debt. Of course, this does not mean we should walk around in rags or that we may not be fashion-conscious or dress properly.

The fourth practice is wisdom. Cultivation of wisdom involves understanding impermanence, realizing that everything is contingent and subject to change. We will go into that later when we start to talk about training in wisdom. Many people say that everything is impermanent, but when Buddhists talk about impermanence, they mean something more than just knowing that things change. The fifth *paramita* is energy. This means that we must have willpower; because if we do not have willpower, if we are suffering from weakness of will, then we can't stop what we should not be doing and we can't do what we should be doing. Without willpower we feel helpless to break through that chain; we feel dependent and the victim of circumstances. So it is very important to develop that sense of willpower or energy.

The sixth virtue that we should be cultivating is patience. Patience obviously means that we should not look for immediate gratification. We should allow time for things to develop and not expect instant results. We should not be too hasty in whatever we do, wanting things to work in a very short period of time. Of course it also means that we should have more tolerance toward disappointments, setbacks, and failures. Just because we fail does not mean we should give up. We should persist in an intelligent and relaxed manner, without being pushy or fixated.

FIVE PRECEPTS (*Pancha-shila*)

That concludes the list of things that we should try to do. Now let us briefly go through the other list of things that we should try not to do, according to the Buddha's moral guidelines. I say "moral guidelines" because according to the Buddha, these precepts are just guidelines, not rigid laws. We should try to stick to them more in terms of the spirit rather than the letter, not thinking that they are inviolable and fixed.

The things that we should abstain from doing are called *panchashila*: *pancha* means "five," *shila* is "conduct." The first precept is abstaining from harming sentient beings. Before we can learn how to love others, first we have to learn how not to harm others. We should not harm any sentient being, and this doesn't mean just human beings, but also animals and even insects. We shouldn't harm them unnecessarily. In Buddhist countries like Tibet, when farmers have to kill insects, they do so with regret, with a sense of feeling for the insects they kill, rather than seeing them as pests ruining their farmlands.

When Buddhists talk about *ahimsa,* or "nonharming," this also includes respect for the environment and biosphere. It means abstaining from harming not only those sentient beings who have self-consciousness, but anything that can grow and prosper and that may be tampered with through human interference. In the teachings it is said that if we develop friendliness, even a venomous snake will respond to it. I was once in Madhya Pradesh in central India, where there is a Tibetan settlement. There were a lot of snakes there. Because of their Buddhist upbringing, the Tibetans didn't kill any snakes, but the local Indians would kill the snakes as soon as they spotted them. What I observed was that the Tibetans were able to wander around safely. In this particular monastery, which at the time was a very temporary kind of shed, snakes would crawl along the beams. Sometimes a monk would be meditating and a snake would come crawling into his lap. The snakes never reacted in an aggressive manner to the monks or to any of the Tibetans, but as soon as they heard Indian voices, either they would try to escape or they would become very aggressive. I don't know whether they have some intelligence, or whether through generations the snakes of that area have developed a biological sensitivity to different inputs. Whatever it is, there was a clear difference. In any case, not harming sentient beings is obviously a good thing.

The second guideline says we should abstain from that which is not given. Apart from taking things by force from others, we sometimes try to procure what we desire through trickery, deception, or sweet talk. For example, if your wealthy grandmother is dying, you start to visit the nursing home more often, hoping that she might leave you something, maybe even everything. We all do that sort of thing, I suppose. It includes generally misleading another person or coercing the person into handing over whatever it is you desire, through threat, manipulation, and trickery.

The third precept is abstaining from sexual misconduct. In Buddhism, sex is not seen as something evil or unnatural in itself. Lay Buddhists can have sexual pleasure and normal sex lives without feeling guilt or fear of punishment. However, a warning is given that if one becomes obsessed with sex, like all obsessions it can cause enormous harm to oneself and others. Once again the real criterion is how much harm one is causing, rather than the sexual act itself. So this should not be misconstrued to mean no sex, or that sex is only for procreation. Abstaining from sexual misconduct means that we should not engage in sexual activities that cause conflict, resentment, or hurt. For example, if we have affairs and this causes pain and suffering to our partner, then it is sexual misconduct and we should refrain from it. But it is made very clear in the Buddhist teachings that what is acceptable and what is not acceptable in terms of sexual and procreative activities varies from culture to culture, and also from individual to individual, so these factors should be taken into account. Fundamentally, it means those sexual activities that cause harm by creating hurt, resentment, bitterness, and disappointment.

The fourth activity that we should abstain from is false speech. Lying is obviously one example of false speech, but there are others, such as spreading rumors, gossiping, backbiting, character assassination, speaking ill of others. It is not lying itself that is evil, but what lying or what false speech can do. We can see the harm it causes. But there are also exceptions. This is why I said that these are moral guidelines only, because one may do more benefit than harm by telling a lie in some exceptional circumstances. The general rule, however, is that lying is something we should refrain from, particularly when the lie is going to cause harm.

The fifth precept is abstaining from alcohol and other intoxicants. Again, alcohol itself is not to blame; but some people who drink alcohol become influenced by it in a way that is destructive both to themselves and others. We know how much of a problem our societies have with drunk drivers, and cases such as people killing their loved ones while in an alcoholic stupor. Alcohol can impair our judgment and cause us to lose consciousness, so that we cannot remember what we did while we were drunk. In the *Vinaya*—the text explaining the rules of life for monks and nuns—when the Buddha talked about abstaining from alcohol and other forms of intoxicants, he told a kind of parable. A monk was out begging for food one day when he came across a woman selling alcohol. She offered him three choices. The first one was to drink alcohol, the second to kill a goat, and the third to have sex with her. He said, "No, I can't kill the goat; a Buddhist monk would never do such a thing. I can't have sex—I'm a monk; I'm celibate. So I'll take the alcohol." He drank the beer, and once he got drunk, he killed the goat and had sex with the woman. The Buddha said that's why alcohol is something we should abstain from, precisely because it can have strange effects on some people.

All the guidelines that we have looked at so far are practical in nature. They give us guidelines for how we should live, what sort of things we should do and what sort of things we should try to refrain from, to increase our own well-being and happiness—lasting happiness, that is—and also to make other people's lives easier. As you can see from this discussion, in Buddhism we do not subscribe to any form of moral absolutism. By this I mean that whatever ethical action we choose, we have to take the situation and a variety of factors into account. We cannot have preconceived notions of right and wrong. Moral absolutists may feel that they know what is right and wrong and, consequently, will not face any form of moral dilemma. Buddhism does not take such a view. For example, abortion may not be a good thing, but in certain circumstances it may be more beneficial to have an abortion than not to have one. If you are starving and have no choice but to steal a loaf of bread, then probably it is more beneficial to steal that bread rather than think, "I subscribe to such-and-such a religious view, which prohibits stealing, so I must allow myself to die rather than steal." In Buddhist ethics we always have to be aware of certain exceptions such as these. Thus, the paramitas are seen not as moral commandments but as moral guidelines.

3

MEDITATION

Changing Our Mental Outlook

Without wisdom and insight, clearly we can never have total self-confidence in what we are doing. With greater insight, we may be able to understand what is truly beneficial and what is truly harmful. Wisdom cannot be developed or cultivated without the practice of meditation, which is the most important part of the Buddhist teachings. It establishes the link between wisdom and ethics or moral conduct. It is through the practice of meditation that we discover which states of mind, emotions, thoughts, and attitudes are beneficial and which are harmful to ourselves and others, and also how these states influence our interaction with other people and the way we live our lives.

If we want to change our behavior, we must have a greater understanding of our own minds and we need to change our attitudes. We also need to change the way we express our emotions. When we do this, we see that negative thoughts and emotions have to be gradually eradicated, not only because they are harmful to others but also because they are fundamentally very harmful to ourselves. That should be the basic motivation for wanting to overcome our negative emotional traits, attitudes, and thoughts.

At a "Mind and Life" conference held in Dharamsala, India, many leading physical scientists, neurologists, psychiatrists, and other specialists met with Buddhist teachers for the purpose of exchanging information. Through reading certain books on Buddhism, these scientists had discovered similarities between Buddhism and their clinical practice. What they had learned was similar to what Buddhists have been saying in relation to how our mental outlook affects our physical health and general well-being.

From a Buddhist point of view, our moral behavior and mental attitudes of necessity have some bearing on our well-being. We refrain from doing certain things not only because they are morally wrong, but because refraining from them fundamentally promotes our well-being. Feelings such as resentment and bitterness gradually make us weak, frustrated, and unhappy, rather than having any impact on the person toward whom we direct these emotions. Probably the other person is away enjoying a nice holiday while we are unable to sleep or eat because we are busy suffering.

When we see how important it is to change our mental outlook, we need a particular technique in order to achieve this. The technique is the practice of meditation. In Buddhism there are two different types of meditation: tranquillity (*shamatha*) and insight (*vipashyana*).

THE MEDITATION OF TRANQUILLITY (*Shamatha*)

The meditation of tranquillity teaches us how to become settled and calm and to concentrate so that our minds are not always reaching out, grabbing on to this and that, and becoming scattered. We learn how to focus our minds, to become centered. We also learn how to be present and not dwell on our past achievements, failures, regrets, or guilt associated with all kinds of things that we may have done or failed to do. Likewise, we learn how not to dwell on or feel anxious about the future: what we would like to achieve, the possibility of not being able to achieve our goals, the imminent obstacles that we can foresee, and so on. We can learn how to be in the present and remain focused. If we indulge in all these mental activities without focus, we lose our perspective and start to react to things more and more from habitual responses rather than from clear understanding. Through the practice of meditation, we can learn how to be attentive and in the present.

As we sit in meditation and a thought or an emotion arises, we let go of it; we try not to dwell on it. At the same time, we do not anticipate the thoughts or emotions that may arise in the future. When we sit, we try to concentrate, usually on the breath. We try not to judge whatever arises in the mind, but simply let it arise and dissipate. As we become more focused, and as we develop a greater ability to remain in a state of concentration, the emotional conflicts that we normally experience begin to subside. When they subside, it becomes possible for wisdom to arise. If the mind is disturbed and distracted, it is impossible to develop wisdom.

The Five Hindrances (Nivaranas)

While we are engaged in the meditation of tranquillity, we must be aware of what are known as the five hindrances. The first one of these is called *sensual desire*. This term alludes to the mind's tendency always to latch on to something that attracts it—a thought, a visual object, or a particular emotion. When we allow the mind to indulge in such attractions, we lose our concentration. So we need to apply mindfulness and be aware of how the mind operates; we don't necessarily have to suppress all these things arising in the mind, but we should take notice of them and see how the mind behaves, how it automatically grabs on to this and that.

The second hindrance is *ill will*; it is the opposite of the first hindrance, being brought about by aversion rather than attraction. Ill will refers to all kinds of thoughts related to wanting to reject, feelings of hostility, resentment, hatred, and bitterness. When they arise, we should take note of them, not necessarily suppressing them but seeing how they arise. At the same time, we should try to practice loving-kindness meditation, which I shall describe shortly.

The third hindrance to meditation is *lethargy and drowsiness*. This is a very familiar one for people who meditate. When this hindrance is present, we lose our focus in meditation. We may not be agitated in any perceptible way, but there is no mental clarity. We gradually become more and more drowsy and then eventually go to sleep. When this happens, instead of persisting with the practice of meditation, it is better to try to refresh ourselves by getting up and going for a walk or washing our face, after which we return to our meditation.

The fourth hindrance is *restlessness and worry*, which refers to all the mental activities that go on in our mind owing to its restless nature. The mind cannot allow us to remain still even for a minute. To counteract this hindrance is once more a matter of applying mindfulness and seeing how the mind behaves, how it reacts to things, and not judging it in terms of what we are experiencing. If we are experiencing something "bad," we should not think that it is bad; if it is "good," we should not think that it is good. We simply take note of what is happening.

The fifth hindrance is called *skeptical doubt* or, as some have translated it, fear of commitment. When we meditate in the presence of this hindrance, we have a constant nagging feeling: "How do I know that I'm doing it right? How do I know that this thing really works and I'm not just wasting my time? How do I know that what the Buddhist teachings say is true? How do I know that what the meditation teachers have taught me is right and that they are not deluded?"

This excessive skeptical doubt has no value and becomes an obstacle to meditation. To work with this hindrance, we should seek to better understand the mind's functioning through reading and trying to broaden our knowledge, instead of indulging in this state of doubt.

Through the practice of tranquillity meditation, we begin to see how our mental attitudes, emotions, and thoughts create the kind of person we are, the character and personality that we have. When we realize this, it is possible to become a different person.

The Four Divine Abodes (Brahmaviharas)

In conjunction with the practice of tranquillity, the meditator is also encouraged to practice what are known as the four *brahmaviharas*. Some translators have rendered these as the four "cardinal virtues of

Buddhism," or as the four "divine abodes." They are: loving-kindness, compassion, sympathetic joy, and equanimity. According to Buddhism, it is not easy for us to become full of loving-kindness or compassion just like that. We have to learn how to do it. We don't seem to have to train ourselves in how to become obnoxious, but it does take a great deal of effort to develop qualities such as loving-kindness.

Some people have said: "Buddhists simply engage in the meditation of loving-kindness—they don't *do* anything." However, the Buddhist view is that if we develop a real sense of loving-kindness and compassion through meditation, then we will be able to express them much more skillfully in the real world. This does not mean that we have to wait until we attain enlightenment before we can be loving. But by trying to think more positive thoughts, gradually we can become more positive in our outlook, and this will have a more positive impact on others.

Loving-kindness (*maitri*) meditation is practiced by sending loving benevolence to specific individuals. When we begin to practice loving-kindness, it is said that the object of that practice should not be a "difficult person," somebody we find hard to get along with, because loving-kindness for that person will not arise naturally. The object of loving-kindness practice should also not be a loved one, because all kinds of distortions may be introduced into the love that we feel for that person. The object of loving-kindness practice should not be someone to whom we feel indifferent, because, again, at this initial stage it is very hard to try to generate love toward someone in whom we have no interest. It is also said that in the beginning we should not try to do this practice with a person of the opposite sex as the object of practice.* So what sort of people are left after that?

According to the teachings, we should first practice loving-kind-

---

*Classic Theravadin texts on meditation such as the *Visudhimagga* and the great Mahayana saint and scholar Shantideva's work *Bodhicharyavatara* devoted substantial attention to contemplation of the ugly, vile, repulsive aspects of the body. Such meditations were practiced not to see sex as being either impure or intrinsically debased, but in order to remove the attraction toward the opposite gender or perhaps toward the same gender. The use of such meditations is viewed as a therapeutic technique.

ness toward ourselves—we are the person whom we should truly try to love, although not in an egocentric manner. From there, we can transfer that feeling to a large group of people who are in need of love, and then gradually try to expand our horizon by including all sentient beings. It is said that we have to do this step by step.

When we try to generate loving-kindness, we have to make sure that it does not become distorted and turn into attachment. Loving-kindness is a really expansive feeling, whereas attachment is narrow and distorts our vision of things. In Buddhism, loving other sentient beings (not just humans, but all sentient beings) is the ultimate kind of love. There is no difference between eros and agape.

The second divine abode is compassion (*karuna*), which is developed when we witness suffering. Beings undergo a variety of sufferings—torture, oppression, all kinds of disadvantages and deprivations. When we witness these things, compassion wells up in our hearts. The word *compassion* literally means "suffering with" others. But in Buddhism, when we feel compassion it is not about suffering with others, but rather seeing the plight they are in and then seeking to alleviate their suffering.

The third divine abode is sympathetic joy (*mudita*), which means that when others are happy, we rejoice with them. We do not feel envy or jealousy at other people's happiness; we feel joy because they feel joy.

The last abode is equanimity (*upeksha*), which is the most important, because without equanimity, loving-kindness can become attachment, compassion can turn into sentimentality, and sympathetic joy can turn into elation. But if we have a proper sense of equanimity, it is possible to keep things in perspective so that our own biases, expectations, and fears do not come in the way of our ability to express these positive emotions. Even with equanimity, however, we must apply mindfulness, because equanimity may turn into indifference, which is actually its opposite. With a sense of equanimity, we are able to do things for ourselves and others, and we can maintain a broader vision; whereas when we are indifferent, we have no interest whatsoever.

THE MEDITATION OF INSIGHT (*Vipashyana*)

So through the practice of the meditation of tranquillity we can learn how to create a tranquil state of mind that is not visibly disturbed. But that in itself is not sufficient. We must learn how to develop insight. The practice of the meditation of tranquillity can make it possible for us to develop insight, but by itself it cannot produce insight. For that we must practice the meditation of insight, or *vipashyana*, beginning with what are known as the four foundations of insight. These are mindfulness of the body, mindfulness of feelings, mindfulness of the mind, and mindfulness of conditioned things. The practice of the meditation of insight relates to obtaining some insight into, or understanding of, the nature of reality, of how things are. When the mind becomes less deluded, and as the obscurations lessen, it is possible to see things more clearly. This includes seeing things as being impermanent and ever-changing, and seeing that nothing has any enduring essence. Through the four foundations of mindfulness, therefore, we can gain insight into impermanence.

With mindfulness of the body, as we begin to observe the body, its sensations, the breath going in and going out, and our experiences on the physical level, we can see the changes that are taking place in the body. The mindfulness of feelings keeps us in touch with the modulations of how we feel, in terms of pain, pleasure, and neutral feelings, and how these feelings are constantly changing. Mindfulness of the mind reveals how unstable the mind itself is, in its thoughts, concepts, and ideas. Lastly, mindfulness of conditioned things means realizing that everything is conditioned and a product of causes and conditions. Nothing can exist by itself, including the mind or our notion of the self. When we think of the self, we think of it as some kind of entity that exists independently of our psychophysical constituents. We talk about "my" body, "my" mind, "my" feelings, "my" perceptions, "my" memory, and so on. Through this practice, as we reflect on our self, for example, we begin to realize that there is no self as an independent entity, that the self is just a collection of physical and mental factors.

We will return to the subject of meditation later, to look at further details of the practice.

4

KARMA AND REBIRTH

Everything Is in Relationship

WE CANNOT COMPLETE OUR DISCUSSION of early Buddhism without including the very important concepts of karma and rebirth. In Buddhism the idea of causality is extremely important. What we mean by causality is that nothing in existence has any kind of enduring essence. Everything is in relationship; everything exists in a dependent manner. Nothing can exist of its own accord. Therefore, everything that exists is causally dependent, either in the physical or mental realm.

That being the case, we must view morality also in terms of causality. Morality is dependent upon the notion of karma, because karma refers to the law of cause and effect in the moral realm. Whatever we do creates certain mental impressions, which in turn produce karmic residues that later come to fruition when the appropriate causes and conditions are present. When we do something positive, wholesome, and good, certain positive impressions are automatically left in the mind. They produce positive and healthy dispositions in us, so that our experiences in the future will be positive and healthy.

When we look at ourselves and at other people, it may not be immediately apparent how this karmic cause and effect operates. For instance, there are good people who do good things and yet they may be experiencing a lot of suffering. They may be ill, disadvantaged, or oppressed. And there are bad people who are nonetheless enjoying a good life. The theory of reincarnation or rebirth is an extension of the concept of karma, which means that we have to look at the whole thing in terms of our previous existence. (I don't like to use the word *incarnation* because it may imply a preexisting psychic substance or soul, and Buddhism does not accept the existence of an eternal soul that incarnates. However, Buddhism believes in a stream of consciousness that gets transferred from one birth to the next. This stream of consciousness is an instance of mental occurrence, arising due to its own internal momentum as well as external stimuli, all of which seemingly perpetuate its continuity over time. It thus serves as the basis for one's self-identity.) Even though a person may not have done anything wrong in this life, that person can have terrible, unwanted experiences because of what he or she has done in a previous life.

Rebirth does not occur in a haphazard way but is governed by the law of karma. At the same time, good and bad rebirths are not seen as rewards and punishments but as resulting from our own actions. That is why in Tibetan the karmic law is called *le gyu dre,* which means "karmic cause and effect." From this we can see how important it is to develop positive and healthy attitudes, because what we do is tied up with the kind of person we are and the kind of mental attitudes we have. We cannot separate these three, because they are intimately related. If we think negative thoughts, we will become negative persons, and if we become negative persons, we will do negative things. For example, if we indulge in aggressive thoughts and harbor resentment or bitterness toward others, we will become an aggressive person. When we indulge in negative or aggressive thoughts, those thoughts have a way of working their way into action, so that we become negative, aggressive people

Without some insight into ourselves and our minds, simply paying attention to what we do will not make us better people in a significant way. For this reason, we should be more attentive to our intentions and attitudes than our behavior or actions.

There is no room in the Buddhist precepts for expressions of moral indignation or outrage. The expressions of unbridled negative emotions such as hatred or disgust toward opponents or those who don't share our own moral worldview are seen as the very root causes of our moral weaknesses. An excessive fixation on "right" and "wrong," the deluded belief that we are on the side of right and good, waging a war against what we perceive as being bad, indulging in or harboring thoughts and emotions that would lead to harmful actions and conduct—all these are to be avoided. Thus, as Buddhists, not only should we engage in good and wholesome actions constantly and consistently, but we should be observant of our inner mental states as well. The Buddha said in the Nikayas (Pali sutras of the early Buddhist canon): "O monks, this I call karma: having had the intention, one acts through body, speech, and mind." So the intention is more important than the action. If our intention is right and sincere and our mind is pure, then even if we do not pay much attention to the actions themselves, we will be able to act in a way that is conducive to the well-being of others, as well as of ourselves.

Even though the happiness, unhappiness, pleasure, or pain that we experience is proportional to our karmic merit or demerit, we should not just accept the situation in which we find ourselves. Buddhism does not encourage a sense of fatalism. Believing in karma does not mean that we should say, "Well, this is my karma, and my karmic lot is so terrible that I can't do anything about it. I'm a loser; I'm a failure." If we find ourselves in an unsatisfactory situation, we should try to improve it or get out of it. There may be a number of options available. Instead of promoting the idea of fatalism, karmic theory actually supports the idea of taking personal responsibility for our actions.

Many of our experiences are not purely a result of karma but are due to our own folly, negligence, or lack of responsibility. For example, if we get sick, obviously we are not going to say, "Well, it's because of my karma that I'm sick, so I'm not going to seek medical attention." We know we should see a doctor and find out what this illness is about. Karmic theory concurs with taking responsibility and wanting to improve the situation, in terms of not only individuals but society as well. Here in the West, people have criticized Buddhists for not being socially aware and not taking social action. They say that people are poor in the East mainly because, in Buddhist countries, they have been taught that it's their karma to suffer and be oppressed, that the situation has nothing to do with social factors and there is nothing they can do to improve it.

However, karmic theory does not say that people should just accept the way things are; we should try our best to change things, to transform ourselves, or to improve social conditions. When our best efforts fail, however, that is the time for us to accept the situation. Suppose that no matter what we do, we still can't change things and there is nothing we can do about it. In such a situation, instead of getting frustrated, angry, or depressed, we should try to learn to live with it. Feelings of enormous psychological stress, anxiety, and suffering simply make things worse. If we feel extremely angry and frustrated about a situation that we can't change, that tends to produce more negative karma, and thus we will experience even more torment and suffering in the future.

To use the example of sickness again, we may have tried everything to combat an illness, but nothing has worked. Then it is better to acknowledge that it is our own karma that has made us ill, and there is no cure. It is better to try to accept the situation than to fight or deny it. Trying to live with that sickness is a much healthier attitude than doing something that is not conducive to our own well-being, such as denying the reality of the illness or having misguided confidence in our powers of recovery.

We should not think of the law of karma in terms of a strict one-to-one causal relationship. There are so many factors involved in our daily circumstances. For example, if I physically assault someone, there will be several factors involved: my intention, my action, and the person whom I have hurt physically. All these factors have a bearing on the karmic consequence that I am going to experience. If the person whom I have struck is a scumbag, as people say, that would be different from hitting a saintly person like Mother Teresa or the Dalai Lama—totally different. Why I hit that person would also have to be taken into account. The law of karma is not so mechanical that if you do a particular action, then invariably a certain effect will manifest. Even if the action is the same, because of these other factors the karmic result may be very different. Thus, the law of karma is not rigid and mechanical but is fluid and malleable.

Good actions, called *kusala* in Pali or *gewa* in Tibetan, are "skillful actions" that produce positive experiences and create healthy dispositions. Bad actions, called *akusala* in Pali or *mi gewa* in Tibetan, are "unskillful actions" that produce a variety of unwanted psychological experiences. In the *Majhimma Nikaya Sutra*, the Buddha describes skillful and unskillful actions in the following manner: "Whatever action—bodily, verbal, or mental—leads to suffering for oneself, for others, or for both, that action is akusala, unskillful action. Whatever action—bodily, verbal, or mental—does not lead to suffering for oneself, for others, or for both, that is skillful action, kusala."

This statement makes it clear that whenever we do something, we should take our own needs and those of others into account. It is not sufficient to think of others' needs alone; nor is it sufficient to take only our own needs into account. There must be a balance. If we think of others' happiness only, we may suffer as a consequence. You may know people who think that they should sacrifice themselves to work for the benefit of others, not thinking about their own benefit. And, of course, there are others, far greater in number, who think that they should do everything possible to promote their own happiness and forget about others. Thus, skillful action means taking both others' needs and our own needs into account, so that they are balanced.

According to karmic theory, we as individuals are responsible for our actions. This responsibility carries over into subsequent lives where we receive compensation, good or evil, for the actions we have performed in previous lives. The psychological or internal effects of these past actions are that they produce certain tendencies and dispositions, which contribute toward the shaping and molding of our personalities. We have the choice of either following these tendencies or, through greater self-knowledge, self-discipline, and self-control, learning how to overcome some of our negative tendencies.

The theory of rebirth is a hypothesis that can explain things that we otherwise find quite difficult to understand. The prevalence of suffering and the injustices that exist in the world—such as innocent people suffering from mental and physical retardation or low social status—can be explained according to karmic theory, without having to appeal to some kind of theological solution. Thus, the "problem of evil" is dealt with very differently in Buddhism and Hinduism than it is in Christianity. Particularly in Buddhism, it is not a theological problem but a moral problem.

The Buddha did not present the theory of rebirth in a dogmatic manner but as a moral wager. He made it clear in the *Majhimma Nikaya Sutra* that believing in rebirth would encourage us to lead a moral life by assuring us of a pleasant and fulfilling future life. However, even if rebirth does not exist, we have not lost anything by believing in it, because leading a moral life makes us into better human beings, endowing this life with meaning and significance.

5

MAHAYANA BUDDHISM

Helping Others Is Helping Oneself

NOW WE SHALL TURN to the later period of Buddhism, known as Mahayana. The Mahayana tradition has two aspects: the Sutra tradition of Mahayana and the Tantra tradition of Mahayana. Mahayana is usually distinguished from early Buddhism, or Hinayana, which literally means "small vehicle." Mahayana is the "large vehicle." The basic point here is that a follower of the Hinayana path has embarked upon a path with a very narrow vision or goal, insofar as that particular person wants to achieve enlightenment for himself or herself alone. That person is not regarded as someone worthy of following the Mahayana path.

When we look at it like that, we should realize that "Hinayana" does not necessarily refer to Theravada Buddhism, as some people assume. After Buddha's demise, Buddhism divided into eighteen sects. One of these was Theravada Buddhism. The sect with which Mahayana was interacting most closely was known as Sarvastivada ("pluralism"), which believed in the ultimate existence of mental and physical entities. When such masters as Nagarjuna and Chandrakirti came on the scene, the school they criticized the most was the Sarvastivadin school. They did not attack Theravadins.

So when Mahayanists today criticize certain tenets of Hinayana, we should not assume that they are attacking Theravada Buddhism as it is practiced today in such countries as Sri Lanka, Myanmar, Thailand, Cambodia, and Vietnam. This is a very important point to make, because the Theravadin tradition is the only one to have survived from the eighteen sects that sprang up following the demise of the Buddha.

Sometimes the word *Shravakayana* is used as a synonym for *Hinayana*. *Shravakayana*, or *nyenthö kyi thekpa* in Tibetan, means the "vehicle of the hearers." *Hinayana,* therefore, does not refer to the allegiance of a practitioner to a particular school but is related to hearing the teachings and assimilating them on an intellectual level, without really practicing them. *Nyen* in Tibetan means "hear," and *thö* means "having assimilated what one has heard on an intellectual level, but not practicing it." So a Shravaka is a person of limited capacity who has not really assimilated the Buddha's teachings.

This clarifies why the Mahayanists have said that people should aspire not to the Hinayana perspective but to the Mahayana, which is also equated with the Bodhisattvayana. A Mahayana follower is also known as a Bodhisattva, the term for someone who, unlike the Hinayana follower, wants to expand his or her vision of spiritual growth. Bodhisattvas do not simply limit themselves to wishing to help themselves; instead, they realize that by helping others, they are in actuality doing something for themselves. That is the ideal, then, of the Bodhisattvayana, or Mahayana.

We see, then, that Hinayana and Mahayana are not determined by doctrines, schools, or belief systems, but by the internal attitude held by practitioners in regard to their spiritual practice. Mahayana practitioners perceive their goal not simply as ridding themselves of suffering, but rather as ridding other beings of suffering. They work for the benefit of others in the understanding that to do something for others is also to do something for oneself.

To give a general outline of the Mahayana teachings, I will talk about the cause of suffering, the path or the method that we must use in order to relieve the cause of suffering, and the fruition that results from practicing the path. The goal of Mahayana Buddhism is no different from that of the early Buddhists. All want to achieve enlightenment. But the quality of the enlightenment, in a sense, is different, because of the motivation. Hinayanists are not necessarily aiming for full enlightenment, but rather for what is known as Arhathood, a state in which one has rid oneself of the emotional conflicts experienced due to anger, jealousy, dissatisfaction, and so forth. In this approach there is no compassion, sensitivity, or a caring attitude.

If we are to follow the Mahayana path, we need to develop an attitude of caring and compassion, because unless we care for others, our development cannot proceed. With that thought, the Mahayana practitioner tries to understand the cause of suffering, and also tries to understand how to rectify that situation. In terms of attitudes toward the cause of suffering, there is no real difference between the Hinayanist and the Mahayanist. The causes of suffering are the two veils of conflicting emotions and conceptual confusion. Conflicting emotions include jealousy, anger, pride, ignorance, and excessive desire. Conceptual confusion relates to the mistaken notion that there is a self with an enduring essence. Hinayanists and Mahayanists both understand that suffering results from not having a proper understanding of oneself and one's emotions.

According to the Mahayana tradition, there is a difference between Hinayana and Mahayana spiritual ideals and the means adopted to realize those ideals. As we said before, Hinayanists are solely concerned with their own well-being and want to achieve enlightenment for their own sake, and thus they do not have the same capacity as Mahayanists. This is not to say that the Hinayana practitioner never thinks of compassion and love. These attitudes may be there, but not to the same extent as with the Mahayanists. Some Buddhist literature emphasizes the importance of self-realization above the practice of compassion toward others, and speaks of the practice of the four brahmaviharas, or divine abodes: loving-kindness, compassion, joy, and equanimity.

Mahayana Buddhism goes further by saying that, if one wants to achieve enlightenment, one needs to do it with a two-pronged approach. The two prongs are compassion and wisdom. One can develop wisdom through the practice of meditation, but one cannot develop compassion by simply meditating on compassion, as is suggested in the four brahmavihara practices. In Mahayana, we have practices such as *lojong*, literally "mental training" but usually rendered as "giving and taking." This series of mental exercises is deployed to gradually break down our rigid, entrenched egocentric thoughts, feelings, and perceptions. In *lojong* we seek to develop compassion by putting ourselves in the place of the deprived or disadvantaged person. But Mahayana says that being compassionate, being helpful, being concerned, and having an altruistic attitude are not sufficient in themselves. We have to engage ourselves with the world. The practice of meditation and the observance of spiritual practices should be undertaken in everyday life, not just in the monastic environment. We have to actually live in the world. This attitude comes from what the Mahayanists say about samsara being identical with nirvana. What does this mean? It means that it is not the world that we have to renounce; it is not that we have to shun all social responsibilities in order to develop spiritually. It is our attitude that is the most important thing. That is why they say that samsara is nirvana. Our delusions are the same as enlightenment, and the world we live in is conditioned by our mind.

Practitioners of Mahayana mainly emphasize the mind and the attitude that we have toward the world, toward other people, and toward ourselves. If we can have a proper attitude, then whatever we do will become wholesome. Instead of thinking that our actions are the most important thing and becoming dogmatic about what is right and what is wrong, with the right attitude we are able to interact with the world in a proper manner. This is the compassionate aspect of the path.

Wisdom, the other aspect of the path, comes from understanding that the self and others are not separate, because everything is interdependent: mind, matter, organic, inorganic—everything that exists in the world is interdependent, and therefore nothing has substantiality. This is taking the teachings of early Buddhism a little further. Early Buddhism says that everything is impermanent, but it does not say that nothing has enduring essence and that everything is interdependent.

Mahayana Buddhism elaborates by saying that everything is interdependent, nothing has self-existence or autonomous status; this is what is meant by emptiness (*shunyata*). Wisdom comes from this realization. If one has a very strong idea of a self-existing (*svabhava*) notion of a self that is completely enclosed within one's body and is divorced from the external world, then one can never be at home in the world. Mahayana Buddhism says that in fact we have already renounced the world as long as we have that belief, because then we are self-enclosed, isolated, and totally divorced from everything else. We perceive the external world as either hostile or something to be exploited and taken advantage of, owing to our desires and our anger.

So if we want to be at home in the world, we need to overcome this way of thinking, and in overcoming it, we attain enlightenment. In order to do that, we need to develop compassion and wisdom. Wisdom is developed through the understanding that the self and others, which we think are totally opposed to each other, are in fact interdependent. The world and the self, the mind and the material world, subject and object, all are interdependent. Once we have that insight, it is easier to develop compassion.

Compassion and wisdom go hand in hand. The Mahayana teachings say that compassion and wisdom should be used like the two wings of a bird. If a bird has only one wing, it cannot fly. In a similar way, if we want to stay aloft, we need wisdom and compassion in the spiritual realm. (We will see later how to develop these two aspects.)

Mahayana Buddhism teaches us how to be in the world without self-deception, without aversion, and without shunning our responsibilities. By facing up to the reality of the situation and realizing that in cultivating wisdom and compassion we are developing ourselves, we see that there is no contradiction. Becoming more compassionate is doing something for ourselves, in actual fact. We do not have to become the doormat for everybody else, or have a self-effacing attitude, or become a "do-gooder." If we act genuinely, with the understanding that can be developed through meditation and wisdom, our compassionate activities in relation to others can lead us to the goal.

That goal, from the Mahayana point of view, is to realize the

physical aspect of Buddha's being through the development of compassion, and to realize the mental aspect of Buddha's being through
the practice of wisdom. I mention this because these things are not
talked about in the teachings of early Buddhism. In the Mahayana
tradition we talk about three aspects of the Buddha's being, which I
will explain later. Here I'm just linking them together by saying that
this is the goal. To gain the physical aspect and the mental aspect of
Buddha's being means that even when one becomes enlightened, one
does not enter into some kind of spirit world divorced from the physical nature of things. Rather, one's own physical body is transformed,
in a sense, due to the mental transformation. From the Mahayana
perspective, mental transformation is the important concept, rather
than mental purification. We aim not to purify the mind but to transform it, because even the mind is not a self-existing, unchangeable
entity.

6

THE WAY OF THE
BODHISATTVA

*Meditation and Action
Go Together*

I HAVE SAID that according to Mahayana Buddhism our delusions lie in two different domains of the mind, one being the emotional aspect and the other being the conceptual aspect. These may also be described as the affective and cognitive aspects of the mind. In relation to the affective aspect of the mind, emotions such as craving, grasping, clinging, hostility, resentment, and bitterness arise. In relation to the cognitive aspect, all kinds of conceptual confusions arise, particularly in our understanding of ourselves—what we think our self or ego is. So there is an interrelationship between the cognitive and emotional aspects of the mind. Generally this view contrasts with the Western understanding, in which it is said that to reason, to have rationality, we must control our emotions. Certain romantics have said that we should eschew rationality altogether because emotion is more valuable than reason. Therefore, those who value rationality often do not value emotions, and vice versa.

But from the Buddhist point of view, the problem of delusion does not emerge purely from one source: either our logical or conceptual abilities or our emotions and feelings. The problem emerges from both of these two sources, and we must have a proper understanding of that.

If that is the problem, then we must find the path by which we can reach the solution. That path has many aspects, but fundamentally it consists of wisdom and compassion. Compassion relates to the emotional aspect, and wisdom relates to the cognitive aspect. Through wisdom we are able to clarify our conceptual confusion and our cognitive distortions; and through compassion we are able to transform our negative emotions.

The ultimate aim of Mahayana Buddhism is not to eradicate emotions as such, but to transform our mind, in both its cognitive and its affective aspects. Finally the path leads to the fruition stage, which also has two aspects—surprisingly enough! Buddhism likes numbers, it seems, and everything is categorized; everything comes in either twos or threes or fives, or some other number. When we simplify the fruition stages of the path, we identify two aspects: the mental aspect of Buddha's being and the physical aspect of Buddha's being. Through the practice of compassion on the path, we are led to the realization of the physical aspect of Buddha's being. Through cultivation of wisdom, we realize the mental or cognitive aspect of Buddha's being. I have already said that, but I want to recapitulate it here.

WHAT IS A BODHISATTVA?

The person who follows the Mahayana path is called a Bodhisattva. The concept of Bodhisattva is found even in early Buddhist literature. For example, in the *Jataka* tales about the Buddha's previous lives before he became awakened, he was referred to in Sanskrit as a Bodhisattva. In Pali literature, the word is *bodhisatta*, and in Tibetan *changchup kyi sempa*. The concept of Bodhisattva is therefore not exclusively a Mahayanist idea or invention. As used in early Buddhism, the word referred to someone who had embarked on the spiritual path and who was progressing toward enlightenment. In Mahayana Buddhism also, the Bodhisattva is not equated with full enlightenment or Buddhahood. The difference is that instead of thinking of Bodhisattvas as being special people with special attributes and abilities, the Mahayanists said that anyone and everyone can become a Bodhisattva. That is why the notion of Bodhisattva became such an important part of Mahayana Buddhism.

The most important characteristic of the Bodhisattva is the element of compassion. Even though compassion was spoken of in relation to the Bodhisattva in early Buddhism, it was Mahayana Buddhism that emphasized this aspect of the Bodhisattva. According to the Mahayanists, enlightenment is not achieved individually by our own effort in a personal kind of way; rather it is achieved in relation to and in interaction with others. Therefore, the element of compassion is emphasized.

So according to Mahayana understanding, when we are being selfish, when we have an acquisitive mentality of wanting more and more—whether it is material goods, fame, love, or whatever—we lose touch with others, we lose touch with the real world. Instead we are living in a world that has been totally created by our own desires, expectations, and frustrations, which does not correspond with the world that is really there.

That is why Mahayana Buddhism talks about overcoming the duality of subject and object, the duality of the mind and the material world. When we develop wisdom, we realize that both subject and object, the mind and the material world, have the same nature. Then, instead of viewing the world as hostile or alien, we see that the world and ourselves are interdependent. And there lies the possibility of developing compassion.

Formal meditation is a solitary journey in which we grapple with our own inner demons and attempt to come to terms with and develop understanding of our own varied psychic forces and states, and this may then lead to the development of wisdom. In order for a spiritual practice to be complete, it must be complemented by compassionate activities in interpersonal situations. In Mahayana Buddhism meditation and activity go hand in hand, in that we cannot really have genuine compassion without wisdom. It is only through developing proper wisdom that we will be able to have compassion and do things for others in a way that is not partial. It does not take very much for us to be compassionate in a partial way. For instance, we can easily feel compassionate toward people whom we like or animals that we cherish. But ideally, from the Mahayana Buddhist point of view, we should aim higher; our compassion should extend even beyond our own dear ones, and that can only be done through wisdom.

If wisdom is not present in compassion, compassion can become degenerated and polluted, owing to our selfishness, sentimentality, or need. I have met people who have a *need* to be compassionate, instead of just *being* compassionate. Compassionate activities should be more like a way of being than a way of doing. Sometimes there are set agendas that accompany the whole idea of performing compassionate acts, so that the most seemingly compassionate people can sometimes also be the most dogmatic. But to be truly compassionate means that we are able to relate with compassion toward a wide variety of people; we don't separate people into good and bad categories, whereby these people on our side are good and need our support, while those on the other side are evil people who are upsetting everything, and therefore we should oppose them. Social activists often run the risk of falling into this attitude. Not that everybody is like that, but sometimes people hold peaceful demonstrations that result in violence.

According to Mahayana Buddhism, when a Bodhisattva meets people who do not share his or her ideas, people who think differently or do things differently, he or she would still try to have an open-minded approach and to communicate in the best way possible to help those beings who may even be hostile. It's important to reiterate that compassion in Buddhism is not something passive. As I pointed out earlier, Westerners regard emotions as being closely related to feelings that we can't help having—just as we can't help it if we have a toothache. Buddhists say that this is not the case with emotions. An emotion like compassion is something active that we can choose to experience and put into action. The fact that we can choose to develop and exercise compassion is significant. As Rollo May states in his book *Love and Will*, if an individual feels powerless to make such choices, it is very difficult for him or her to love and have compassion. The only way to overcome that sense of powerlessness is to learn how to love and how to generate compassion. Buddhists would agree with that.

Compassion should not have anything to do with suffering with and for another, but should instead arise from the intention to alleviate another's suffering. Mahayana literature defines love or lovingkindness as the wish that others may have happiness and the causes of happiness; compassion is defined as the wish that others may be free from suffering and the causes of suffering. Those are very general definitions, but they show that this is an active form of doing something, rather than allowing ourselves to become immersed in other people's misfortune or despair. If we identify too much with others' suffering, our own ability to help those others becomes diminished. Psychotherapists have also made this point: therapists who overidentify with the problems of their clients may find that their ability to help the clients is reduced. This is precisely because the therapist is totally absorbed in the whole dynamic of the situation.

Two Kinds of Bodhisattva

There are two different kinds of Bodhisattva: the ideal Bodhisattva and the Bodhisattva who aspires to achieve enlightenment. "Ideal Bodhisattvas" are part of the Buddhist pantheon. In Mahayana, unlike in early Buddhism, we have many different images of realized beings, both mythological and real. The mythological Bodhisattvas in particular are seen as models who embody certain qualities of the Bodhisattva. So we talk about Bodhisattvas such as Avalokiteshvara (called Chenrezik in Tibetan), Manjushri, and Vajrapani. A Bodhisattva such as Avalokiteshvara embodies compassion and is used as an example of how one can develop compassion. It is not that we must believe in Avalokiteshvara as a real being; rather we use the image of Avalokiteshvara to think about how we might develop this ideal of compassion in ourselves. Similarly, Manjushri embodies wisdom. Through visualizing Manjushri and doing practices related to Manjushri, we can try to emulate the qualities that Manjushri possesses. Vajrapani embodies the quality of will, so his image can be used as an antidote against apathy, to increase our ability to follow this path. The Bodhisattva of Achala (whose name means "nonmoving") is the embodiment of samadhi, or the meditative state. By visualizing all of these Bodhisattvas and by emulating them, we are using them as antidotes to our habitual tendencies. In this way, Manjushri becomes the antidote to ignorance, Avalokiteshvara to selfishness, Vajrapani to apathy, and Achala to the distracted or agitated mind. These are the ideal Bodhisattvas.

The other type of Bodhisattva corresponds to the idea that everyone has the ability to become enlightened, to become a Bodhisattva. These two kinds of Bodhisattva should be distinguished, because it can be especially confusing for newcomers who are told that there are these Bodhisattvas who are supposed to be realized, and then one is also told to emulate the Bodhisattva behavior and become a Bodhisattva oneself. The Bodhisattvas who are ideal images already embody all the qualities of the Bodhisattva, or at least some of them. But those who belong to the second type of Bodhisattva need to cultivate the qualities they do not have. Within this second group there are two kinds: those who have already embarked upon the Bodhisattva path, and others who are potential Bodhisattvas, so that if the right circumstances arise they may actually become Bodhisattvas.

BECOMING A BODHISATTVA

So how does one become a Bodhisattva? There is just one necessary and sufficient condition, which is to generate *bodhichitta,* or the "heart of enlightenment." *Bodhi* means "enlightenment," and *chitta* means "heart."

Bodhichitta also has two aspects, one being the relative aspect and the other being the ultimate aspect. *Ultimate* bodhichitta refers to the nature of the mind itself, or what we call Buddha-nature. (We'll come to a discussion of that later.) *Relative* bodhichitta is the cultivation and generation of compassion. In order to develop this, it is not sufficient to just think, "From now on, I will try to do my best to generate compassion and overcome my egocentricity, because it is not only beneficial for others but is also beneficial for myself." We have to make a formal commitment, which is called the taking of the Bodhisattva vow. As we know, living with somebody for many years in a de facto relationship is different from signing on the dotted line. Somehow that makes a difference; I suppose it is because when we make a formal commitment in public rather than simply saying something to ourselves mentally, there is an aspect of promise about it. And when we promise something, there may be more of a chance that we will follow through. So bodhichitta is aroused by making a formal commitment.

After making such a commitment, the Mahayana teachings say, the Bodhisattva should not be in a hurry to attain enlightenment. We have the ability to actually postpone our own enlightenment as long as necessary, because as Bodhisattvas we feel that it is better for others to achieve enlightenment before we do ourselves. We have no sense of urgency and can say, "I will work for the benefit of others; I want others to attain enlightenment before I do."

In some of the books on Buddhism written by Western scholars and practitioners, there is a problem with this idea. For example, Peter Harvey, the author of *An Introduction to Buddhism*, questions: if a Bodhisattva is not the same as a Buddha, how is it possible for such a person to lead others to a state of enlightenment, even if he or she has the desire to do so? The Bodhisattva may be deluded in thinking that he or she has the ability to do so, but to be able to lead others to enlightenment entails the possession of certain abilities. Paul Williams's book *Mahayana Buddhism* poses a different question: is it not problematic to talk about the postponement of enlightenment? For then it raises the possibility that it might be better not to embark upon the Bodhisattva path, if by embarking upon it others will attain enlightenment while you, as the Bodhisattva, still remain in the samsaric condition.

The point is not to take all these statements so literally but to understand them in relation to attitude. By developing the infinite compassion that a Bodhisattva is able to develop, one brings enlightenment closer, whereas without that kind of compassion, enlightenment is far off. Even if one desperately wants to become enlightened, one is unable to do so.

Chögyam Trungpa Rinpoche gave a very graphic image of this. He said that embarking on the Bodhisattva path in a proper way is like being in a vehicle that is preprogrammed to take you to your destination even if you don't want to go there. I think it is like that. If you have the right attitude, then you attain enlightenment in spite of yourself. That really is the Mahayana attitude as it is transmitted orally. But if you become fixated on the texts in which it is not explicitly stated that this is how one approaches the Bodhisattva path, you may take the whole thing too literally.

Shantideva says in the first chapter of the *Bodhisattvacharyavatara*: "May I become a shelter for the homeless; may I become food for the hungry; may I become a bridge for those who want to cross the turbulent waters." Obviously Shantideva is not wishing to be a magician so that he can literally become these things.

Having said that, I should add that what this really means is that doing compassionate activities for others should go beyond physical activities, such as feeding the hungry. Of course, wherever possible, we should try to do those things. But wherever it is impossible to actually do this, we should not think, "A mere mental attitude will not alleviate others' suffering if I haven't got the physical means to do so. My effort will have no effect, so it's a waste of time." We should not give up the practice. Wishing that the Ethiopians, for example, were relieved of their suffering could have an enormously beneficial effect, even though physically nothing has changed for the Ethiopians. It is the attitude that really is the most important thing. If we have the right attitude, arising from wisdom, whatever action we initiate out of compassion will be effective and will be in keeping with the situation. But if we lack such an open and wide vision, even if we are very concerned with social welfare and justice, our attitude may still be tinged or polluted with our own delusions or obscurations of mind.

7

REALIZING WISDOM AND COMPASSION

Bodhichitta and the Paramitas

WE HAVE SEEN that the concept of the Bodhisattva in Mahayana Buddhism is of the ideal image of a spiritual practitioner, which all followers should try to emulate. Now let us look in more detail at how the Bodhisattva way of life is accomplished.

In chapter 6, I briefly mentioned generating bodhichitta, or enlightened heart. Bodhichitta has two aspects: the absolute aspect refers to the nature of the mind already inherent in all living beings, and the relative aspect refers to compassion. The first of these, the absolute aspect, is related more to wisdom, while the relative aspect is related more to compassion. If we want to obtain enlightenment by becoming a Bodhisattva, it is necessary to actualize wisdom and compassion. This is done by the practice of what are called the six *paramitas*, or "transcendental actions."

Para in Sanskrit literally means the "other shore." Here it means going beyond our own notion of the self. From the Buddhist point of view in general, and from the Mahayana point of view in particular, if we want to progress properly on the path, we need to go beyond our conventional understanding of the self. So when we say that *paramita* means "transcendental action," we mean it in the sense that actions or attitudes are performed in a non-egocentric manner. "Transcendental" does not refer to some external reality, but rather to the way in which we conduct our lives and perceive the world— either in an egocentric or a non-egocentric way. The six paramitas are concerned with the effort to step out of the egocentric mentality. In this chapter I shall discuss the first four paramitas (generosity, moral precepts, patience, and vigor), which are all concerned with our physical actions and are related to the moral domain. The practice of the last two paramitas (meditation and wisdom) is concerned with the mind, and these paramitas are the subject of chapter 8.

GENEROSITY (*Dana*)

The first paramita is *dana* in Sanskrit, which means "generosity." The *Bodhisattva-bhumi*, a very important Mahayana text, defines it as "an unattached and spontaneous mind, and the dispensing of gifts and requisites in that state of mind." The essence of generosity is giving without any attachment or expectations, without thought of receiving something in return. It is doing something purely for its own sake, with no strings attached.

In the Mahayana tradition, generosity has three aspects. The first is practicing generosity on the material level. This means that we are able to extend ourselves and not hesitate to help people in need, and that we don't become so attached to our possessions that we cannot share them. This type of generosity works on the physical level by relieving people's physical pain and deprivation.

The second aspect is practicing generosity by giving protection, by protecting people's lives. This means that if others are in danger, we do not hesitate to help them; we do not hold back. If a person is caught in a burning house, we must act to save that person. If we suspect that the child next door is being abused, we don't think that the child isn't ours and therefore we have no responsibility; we act to protect the child.

The point, at least for Bodhisattvas, is that we should do whatever it takes in any given moment to save a life. This extends even further, because it is not only human life that needs to be saved but the lives of all sentient beings. So if a modern Bodhisattva here in Australia, where I live, is driving along the road and accidentally hits a kangaroo, he or she doesn't just "shoot through," as they say, but stops to do something to save that animal's life. Giving protection is called the generosity of fearlessness.

The third type of generosity is that of giving spiritual teachings and advice. In the Mahayana literature it is clearly stated that there are three aspects to this: the first is the object of generosity, the person to whom we might direct such teachings. This person needs to be interested in receiving teachings or advice. If someone is not interested, then no matter how much we talk, no matter how much we want to give advice, nothing will be achieved. So we don't go around saying, "Avon calling!" People may say, "Go away, I don't want to listen to you!" Why then should we persist? But if a person is open-minded, then the situation is workable. So the object or person to whom the teachings are directed should be kept in mind.

The second aspect is the intention. When we want to impart teachings or give advice, we must do it with a pure intention, not sullied by thinking that we are better or know more than the person we are trying to help. The teacher's motivation should be pure and free from delusions.

The third aspect is the way of imparting the Dharma. In the *Bodhisattva-bhumi*, Asanga says: "To make a gift of the Dharma means to explain it logically and not in a perverted way, and to make the disciple hold firmly to the principle of training therein." We should give spiritual advice to others in a coherent manner, logically and eloquently, and in a way that does not give rise to strong emotional reactions, as these would only increase the delusions already present in the people receiving teachings.

MORAL PRECEPTS (*Shila*)

The second paramita is called *shila* (Tibetan, *tsültrim*), or ethics. A better translation would be "moral precepts," because all the paramitas are involved with ethics or morality, not just shila. The distinctive feature of shila paramita is that it is involved with the taking of certain precepts. In the Mahayana tradition, it is said that without precepts we are like a person without feet—we cannot get a foothold, we cannot stand upon the ground. As a Mahayana sutra says: "Just as you cannot walk without feet, so also can you not become liberated if you lack ethics or moral precepts." In Tibetan, tsültrim is always referred to as *tsültrim che kangpa*, which means "foot of moral precepts." So shila is seen as the foundation, that which grounds us in spiritual practice or connects us to the earth.

The paramita of moral precepts has three aspects. The first is related to restraint, as in the precepts against killing and lying. It is important not to yield to such impulses and act on them; we must exercise some form of restraint.

The second aspect of the precepts is "gathering of wholesomeness," which means that it's not sufficient simply to restrain oneself from negative forms of actions; having exercised restraint, one must then engage in positive deeds. For this reason one is counseled to engage in wholesome mental attitudes such as contemplation on love, compassion, and affection, and try not to get engrossed in negative emotions such as bitterness, resentment, hostility, and hatred. The term in Tibetan is *gewa chödü; gewa* means "wholesome" and *chödü* means "gathering." So we gather all that is wholesome and positive within ourselves.

The third aspect of the precepts is acting to benefit others, not just ourselves. What distinguishes the Mahayana idea of precepts is this emphasis on benefiting others. In the Mahayana tradition, however, the precepts are not to be followed blindly; they have nothing to do with rules and regulations. It is a Mahayana idea that there is no such thing as absolute moral principles. Precepts should be followed skillfully rather than blindly, which is connected with the Mahayana idea of *upaya,* "skillful means."

Moral precepts should also not be followed out of fear of punishment or hope of reward. This is made very clear in another sutra: "Moral precepts are not to be observed for the sake of kingship, the bliss of heaven, or the position of Indra, Brahma, or Ishvara [that is, to attain the powers of gods]; nor for the enjoyment of wealth, nor the world of forms and other experiences. They are not to be observed out of the fear of hell, of rebirth among animals or the world of Yama. On the contrary, ethics or moral precepts are to be observed in order to become like Buddhas and to bring happiness or profit to all beings." Mahayana Buddhists would say that following moral precepts for reward or out of fear may, in fact, turn out to be an immoral act.

PATIENCE (*Kshanti*)

The next *paramita* is patience (*kshanti*), which is seen as the antidote to anger, frustration, resentment, hostility, and the like. An impatient mind becomes a victim of these emotions. As Shantideva says in the *Boddhisattvacharyavatara*: "When one adopts an attitude tinged with the sting of malevolence, the mind does not experience peace. Since one does not find joy and happiness, one becomes sleepless and restless." If there is hatred in the mind so that it is dominated by feelings of resentment and anger, then it becomes restless and, as Shantideva says, we cannot even sleep properly. Shantideva goes on to say: "In brief, there is no such thing as anger in happiness; so when we feel happy, there is no anger. Anger and happiness cannot coexist."

If we are to overcome suffering—which is the ultimate aim of Buddhism—we must overcome negative tendencies in the mind, because positive states of mind such as peace and happiness cannot coexist with negative tendencies. Therefore, it is important to develop patience. It is not enough just to recognize the harmful effects these negative tendencies have on our lives. We need to actively practice patience to overcome them.

Shantideva also says: "There is no such thing as anger in happiness; a person's friends tire of him, and even though he entices them by generosity, they do not stay." For as long as we do not change our ways, we may try to bribe people with gifts to show our affection, but they won't be duped and will cease to be our friends. So anger has all kinds of negative consequences, not only in relation to our spiritual practice but also in our life generally.

The practice of patience has three aspects. The first concerns coping with harmful people; the second, working with difficult situations; the third, investigating the whole of reality. First, the Bodhisattva has to learn how to cope with people who have very difficult personalities, who are aggressive, annoying, and upsetting. According to many Mahayana teachings, the best way to do this is to realize that, if someone is completely overpowered by anger, we should think of that person as being like someone who is mentally unstable or under the influence of alcohol and therefore not fully in control. If we act in the same way this other person does, we cannot solve anything. So we need to review the situation properly and act sensibly.

The second aspect relates to working with difficult situations. Even when we are confronted with these, we should not yield to despair or frustration. We need to realize that life is not easy, that difficulty is part of life; we should not think that everything will go smoothly or fall into our laps just like that, without our making any effort. When difficulties arise, we should try to exercise patience and tolerance, keep our mind lucid, and not be influenced by despair and hopelessness.

The third aspect is called "investigating the whole of reality," which will be discussed later as part of the paramita of wisdom. What this means, in brief, is that the Bodhisattva should have the understanding that everything takes place because of causes and conditions. Difficulties that we experience are not permanent, because everything depends upon causes and conditions and is transient. Therefore, we need not become so fixated on or obsessed by the problems we experience at any given moment.

Vigor (*Virya*)

The next paramita is called *virya,* often translated as "effort"; but I think "vigor" is better, because "effort" makes it sound like plain hard work! But if we have vigor, we do not need to make any effort. For example, we may have to make an effort to put the garbage out, whereas a person with vigor would do this effortlessly. With vigor we do not flinch or get bogged down or dragged down; we don't run out of energy.

One Mahayana sutra says: "Unsurpassable perfect enlightenment is not difficult for those who make the effort, because where there is effort, there is enlightenment." Even to gain enlightenment, if there is vigor, it is not so difficult. If there a sense of vigor, enthusiasm, and energy, things are not that difficult. Another sutra says: "Enlightenment is easy for the hard-working." What these quotations make clear is that, if we put our mind to it, we will achieve results. If Bodhisattvas put their mind to achieving enlightenment, that goal is not so far away, and this is true for all of us.

The paramita of vigor acts as an antidote to laziness. In the teachings there are three types of laziness: the first is laziness resulting from inactivity or lack of interest, thinking that you can't be bothered. You may ask, "What's the point? Why do anything?" So you remain in bed for three days in a row, dirty dishes pile up, and so on. The second kind of laziness comes from lack of confidence, from thinking, "How could a person like me achieve anything? Even if I tried, it wouldn't work." Failure is anticipated even before it has happened. With this attitude we preempt any kind of success we might have. The last kind of laziness has to do with overactivity, always being busy, doing this and that, working at three different jobs. When you have nothing to do, you make a telephone call or you visit somebody, out of a constant restlessness that prevents anything from being accomplished. We need to practice the paramita of vigor in order to overcome our tendency toward these kinds of laziness.

There are three different types of vigor as well. The first is called "armorlike vigor." This means that we consciously make the decision that, until we attain our goal, we will not allow ourselves to be sidetracked. This decision is made with fortitude, so there is no distraction.

The second is the "vigor of applied work," and this relates to our physical aspect. Having made such a commitment, we need to engage in *upaya*, or skillful means. When interacting with others, a Bodhisattva has to be very skillful; certain negative tendencies can have a narrowing effect, while positive tendencies have an opening-up effect. Some behavioral attributes may appear to be so similar that initially we cannot differentiate them clearly. But with practice a Bodhisattva is able to discern the differences. For example, arrogance and self-confidence may appear similar, but they are actually quite different. Arrogance narrows one's vision, whereas self-confidence can be uplifting and expansive. Aggression may be seen as self-assertiveness and attachment as affection; indifference may be confused with being dispassionate and self-indulgence mistaken for self-reflection. Gradually, through interaction with others and the practice of the paramitas, Bodhisattvas come to understand what is skillful and beneficial in dealing with others.

The last aspect of vigor or effort is "discontentedness." Buddhism frequently speaks of overcoming dissatisfaction and discontentment, as if these experiences are always undesirable. In certain respects, however, discontentment is necessary. No matter what we have achieved in the past about which we may justifiably feel proud, we should not be satisfied with that but should look to develop and improve ourselves further. This is an ongoing process. We should have the enthusiasm to want to go further and further in relating to others and developing ourselves on a spiritual and psychological level. Our normal experiences of dissatisfaction, incompleteness, deprivation, privation, or sense of lack can and must be sublimated into spiritual ones. We should never be satisfied with our spiritual progress, thinking, "This will do," or "That is enough." We should always have hunger for deeper, higher, richer experiences on the path.

8

The Link between Wisdom and Compassion

The Paramita of Meditation and the Nine Stages of Shamatha

The Mahayana idea of the six paramitas is not so different from the Eightfold Noble Path of early Buddhism. Both practices emphasize cultivating compassion and wisdom, achieved through the three trainings of shila, samadhi, and prajna—morality, meditation, and wisdom. Through developing our morality we can arouse compassion, and through meditation we are able to cultivate insight or wisdom.

If a practitioner engages in meditation and develops wisdom but is unable to develop compassion, a problem arises. Through wisdom we may be able to understand the nature of the self and to have a certain understanding of reality, but without compassion we are unable to be in the world and interact with other living beings. Similarly, compassion without wisdom may enable us to interact with other living beings, but our lack of wisdom causes that interaction to become polluted with defilements, delusions, and illusions.

The paramita of meditation is the link between wisdom and compassion. To practice the first four paramitas in a non-egocentric manner is very difficult without the practice of meditation. It is also true that, without the practice of meditation, it is nearly impossible to develop wisdom. So meditation is the key to self-development and making advancement on the spiritual path.

In the West, what meditation means and the reasons for practicing it are understood in many different ways. Meditation has become quite popular. Many people, particularly in the health professions, now recognize its benefits. Some people think that meditation will help them live longer, prolong their youth, lose weight, stop smoking, and so on. Meditation may do all those things, but in the Eastern traditions, such as Buddhism and Hinduism, it has a more profound meaning. Meditation is not practiced for a specific reason such as reducing stress, increasing concentration while playing sports, or dealing with anxiety. It has to be put in the overall context of how we view our lives and how we perceive the world; this can only be provided by a certain kind of philosophical or religious perspective.

Many people are frightened by the notion of religion and say, "I want to learn how to practice meditation, but please spare me the Eastern mumbo-jumbo. I am quite willing to do the breathing exercises or whatever else you tell me to do." In the Eastern tradition, the practice of meditation relates to transforming ourselves in a fundamental way, not simply changing one aspect of our self. By transforming ourselves we are able to deal with whatever happens in our lives in an appropriate and a meaningful way.

Meditation is *samadhi* or *dhyana* in Sanskrit, and *samten* in Tibetan. In Chinese it has been translated as *ch'an,* and in Japan it is more commonly known as *zen*, which is a corruption of the Chinese term. *Samten* in Tibetan basically means "stable mind." *Sam* can mean either "mind" or "thinking," and *ten* means "stable." The mind that does not easily become distracted, that can remain focused and concentrated, is in meditation. In the West meditation can refer to thinking or pondering on a problem, but in Eastern traditions it refers to the undistracted mind, which is able to focus on the object of meditation.

We saw in chapter 3 that there are two different types of meditation in Buddhism. The meditation of tranquillity, or *shamatha* in Sanskrit, is called *shi-ne* in Tibetan, which means "dwelling in peace."

Insight meditation, or *vipashyana* in Sanskrit, is *lhakthong* in Tibetan, meaning "superior seeing."

We start with the shamatha aspect, or meditation of tranquillity, because without tranquillity, insight cannot be developed. Sometimes insight meditation is also translated as "analytical meditation," which may suggest it has something in common with what we normally mean by meditating on a particular problem. But although it does involve the use of thoughts and concepts, these are considered in the light of how such thoughts and concepts arise in the mind.

In tranquillity meditation we do not concern ourselves with thought and concepts. This is not to say that we should reject or suppress them. We should take note of them as they arise, realizing that they are present, and then try to let go of them. We do not use thought in tranquillity meditation as we do in insight meditation. We need to understand from the beginning which attitudes hinder or help our progress in tranquillity meditation.

PRINCIPLES OF PRACTICE

Shamatha meditation itself has no single practice; instead there is quite a diversity of approaches. According to the Buddhist traditions generally, as part of creating the proper condition for tranquillity to arise, it is important for the meditator to restrain the senses, fondness for food, and anything else that has the potential to disturb or befuddle the mind. While maintaining this kind of composure, the meditator should settle himself or herself comfortably by adopting what is called "Vairochana nine-point posture." This is recommended as the most beneficial meditation posture. It is a cross-legged position, with hands resting one on the other in the lap or resting on the knees, shoulders slightly stretched, head slightly inclined forward, spine absolutely straight like an arrow, gaze directed downward and concentrating on the tip of the nose, mouth slightly open, the tip of the tongue touching the roof of the mouth, and the breathing even and relaxed. The implication is that one should resist and desist from introducing modifications to the posture. This may be an important point, in view of the fact that so many Westerners have started to adapt meditation postures to suit their own preferences. Perhaps in this case an individual's own preferences should not be given consideration (unless, of course, there is a debilitating physical constraint of some kind).

Having adopted the posture of Vairochana, the meditator then should focus his or her mind on the breath. It does not have to be the breath; we could use other objects of concentration, such as an image of the Buddha. However, the use of the breath for this purpose is seen by all Buddhists, regardless of tradition, as the most practical and most effective option. One should breathe naturally, without effort, and avoid breathing either loudly, with undue stress and strain, or in a very shallow manner. If the meditator persists with shamatha by learning to coordinate the breath, his or her mind will gradually become more tranquil and settled.

In the course of shamatha meditation, the meditator needs to become familiar with the use of what are known as the antidotes. These antidotes are used to counteract certain known obstacles to meditation. So at this point the meditator has to know what these obstacles are, and what the anitidotes to them are as well. When should we resort to the antidotes, and when should we desist from using them? Knowing when to use the antidotes is as important as knowing when not to use them.

OBSTACLES TO MEDITATION

There are five obstacles or faults, eight antidotes, and nine stages that apply to tranquillity meditation. (The five obstacles of Mahayana are different from the five hindrances that we discussed in chapter 3 in relation to early Buddhism.) The first fault is laziness; the second, forgetfulness; the third, drowsiness and mental agitation; the fourth, nonapplication; and the fifth, overapplication. Of the eight antidotes, four of them are for the obstacle of laziness: conviction, inclination, exertion or vigor, and pliancy of body and mind. To deal with the second obstacle, forgetfulness, we use the antidote of mindfulness. The third obstacle, drowsiness and agitation (these are counted as one), has the antidote of awareness. The fourth obstacle is nonapplication, for which the antidote is obviously application. The fifth obstacle is overapplication; in order to counteract that, we resort to the antidote of equanimity.

The *Madhyanta-vibhanga* says: "All aims may be realized by settling in tranquillity and making the mind pliant through abandoning the five faults by employing the eight antidotes. Settling the mind in tranquillity is the cause, tranquillity is the effect. Remembering the benefit of tranquillity, detecting laziness and agitation, abandoning faults or obstacles, applying antidotes, reaching intrinsic tranquillity—these are the eight antidotes." This text uses slightly different terms to express the importance of being able to deal with these five obstacles by the application of the eight antidotes. Meditators who have not developed the ability to detect the obstacles, or who have detected the obstacles but have not been able to use the antidotes, are robbed of the experience of tranquillity.

Laziness

There are three types of laziness, the first obstacle. The first gives rise to self-defeating attitudes, such as thinking that we do not have the ability to improve ourselves through our own effort. We think the obstacles are so overwhelming that it is impossible to make any progress on our own. The second type of laziness is that which arises from habitual patterns. Even if we have the desire to meditate and realize that it is very useful, because we are used to a certain way of life, or because of the company that we keep or the kinds of internal propensities that may be present, we may not be able to overcome these obstacles. The third obstacle is the lack of interest. We think, "What is the point of meditating? It is not really going to change things very much, and afterwards I will still be the same." In this way of thinking, meditation may be perceived as a waste of time.

In order to overcome these three types of laziness, we apply four different antidotes. The first is conviction, which means we reflect on our situation and think about the benefits of meditation. We look at the continuing harm we could create by not meditating and realize how much suffering is generated through lack of mindfulness and awareness. For example, we could look at how, in a moment of anger, we reacted to people or situations in a way that we later regretted, wishing that we could have stopped ourselves.

In Buddhism we talk about three gates through which we create karmic effects: body, speech, and mind. We can realize how much harm has been created due to lack of mindfulness, whether physical, verbal, or mental. If mindfulness and awareness had been present, we might not have had to regret the destructive things we have done, said, and thought. Many psychologists now call extreme anger, hostility, and jealousy "toxic emotions." In Tibetan Buddhism such emotions are called poisons, so the meaning is similar.

People today can get very confused about emotions, because we are sometimes told that it is good to assert ourselves and "be somebody." On the other hand, when we act in an aggressive manner, we may be chastised and put down for it. The same can be said of jealousy. In some situations, if we do not show jealousy, our partners may accuse us of not loving them enough. But in another situation, a display of jealousy may elicit accusations of possessiveness. All of these emotions can have a toxic effect, and it is important to realize how we can control them through the practice of meditation, by becoming focused and attentive. So we need to develop conviction, the first antidote. Conviction can arise only if we are convinced of the benefits of meditation and of the harm that conflicting emotions cause in a distracted, confused mind.

Once conviction has been developed, we must follow that up with the cultivation of what is called inclination. If we have real conviction that meditation works and that we must maintain it as part of our practice, then the inclination to want to practice arises more naturally than if we lacked conviction and approached meditation in a half-hearted manner. When inclination is present, the third antidote for laziness—vigor—can be applied. When there is conviction and inclination, it is not difficult for us to be enthusiastic about the practice of meditation, and a sense of vigor easily arises as a result of developing inclination.

This whole process leads to the final antidote, which is pliancy of body and mind. When we do not meditate, the mind and body can become rigid. The posture and facial expression are rigid, the muscles are taut and tense, and the mind is consequently also very rigid and inflexible. Through the practice of meditation and applying the anti-dotes, the body and mind will become flexible. This is conducive to developing a tranquil state of mind.

Forgetfulness

The second obstacle or fault is forgetfulness, the antidote for which is mindfulness. This is first developed through focusing the mind on an external object. Meditators are commonly advised to use a small object, such as a pebble or a piece of wood, and attention is anchored to that object. After a period of time, the focus of attention can be switched to the breath. At the beginning this can be done by counting the breath—counting up to five, fifty, or whatever—then going back and starting all over again, repeating that again and again. Eventually the mental processes of thoughts and emotions that arise in the mind can be used as objects of meditation. In all these cases, the most important thing is not to forget to return to the object of meditation when we realize that we have become distracted or have lost attention. As soon as we have that realization, we should try to make an effort to return to the object of meditation. Of course, we can practice mindfulness in everyday life as well—while driving, washing the dishes, taking the dog for a walk. If we are able to focus our minds on whatever we are doing, that is seen as part of the practice of meditation.

Drowsiness and Agitation

The third obstacle or fault is drowsiness or dullness and agitation, and these two are counted as one. To counteract these two tendencies, we apply awareness. As we begin to develop and cultivate mindful-ness regarding external objects, by focusing our minds on the breath, on our mental processes, and so on, it becomes possible to practice awareness. Without mindfulness it is almost impossible to be aware of these two fundamental obstacles to meditation, dullness or drowsi-ness and mental agitation. Even if no particularly disturbing thoughts are arising in the mind, or no strong, violent emotions are present, and there is a semblance of calmness, nevertheless there is no real sense of clarity. The mind is dull, which can lead to a feeling of drowsiness or stupor. This is harder to detect than mental agitation, the incessant inner chatter and dialogue and the upsurge of emotions that can disrupt our meditative state. Awareness should be applied to detect whether dullness or mental agitation is present.

Nonapplication and Overapplication

The fourth obstacle is nonapplication, which means being unable to apply the antidotes: four in relation to laziness, one in relation to forgetfulness, and one in relation to dullness and agitation. We need to exert ourselves in making use of these antidotes wherever they are appropriate.

The fifth obstacle is overapplication. After having practiced for a certain period of time, we may find that, even when it is unnecessary, out of habit we still use the antidotes rather than letting the mind be in a natural state of tranquillity. Therefore, the antidote of equanimity should be used here.

This is how the eight antidotes relate to the five faults or obstacles. Obviously the practice of meditation is a very long, arduous process; it may not always be very pleasant and does not necessarily lead to an enduring experience of bliss. As Saraha, the famous Indian *mahasiddha* (tantric yogin), has said: "When I apply great effort and hold on tight to the object, I become agitated; when I use less effort, I am overcome by dullness. It is very difficult to balance these two tendencies. When I engage in meditation, my mind becomes disturbed." So it is always a question of trying to strike a balance when applying the antidotes. Meditation is about learning how to apply the antidotes when necessary and not applying them too much or when they are not really necessary. This is something we have to find out on our own.

THE NINE STAGES OF SHAMATHA

The five obstacles and eight antidotes are related to the nine stages of shamatha. The first stage is called "resting the mind." In the beginning, we are constantly grappling with obstacles on the one hand and the use of antidotes on the other. Gradually we may be able to rest the mind for a short period of time, before obstacles arise and disrupt that meditative state. Owing to lack of experience, we may not be able to use the antidotes effectively and may therefore find it very difficult to actually return to the object of meditation. Fantasies, emotions, and thoughts may overwhelm us, making it very difficult. But through consistent effort, we will arrive at the next stage, which is called "continuous resting."

At this stage we develop a greater ability to apply mindfulness and awareness, so that when the obstacles arise, we can return to the object of meditation rather than becoming overwhelmed by them. In both the first and second stages, laziness is the predominant obstacle, characterized by a lack of interest, a lack of inclination toward meditation, or a lack of conviction about the benefits of meditation. Meditators should constantly contemplate these things. We should reflect on our lives and our life experiences, on how we suffer because of our erroneous, distorted thoughts and negative, conflicting emotions.

The third stage of the meditation of tranquillity is called "repeated resting" of the mind (sometimes translated as "patch-like resting"). On this level, not only do we have a greater ability to use mindfulness, but we also have developed skills in dealing with the major obstacles of dullness and agitation. Being able to stay with the object of meditation is only the first step; being aware of the fundamental obstacles of dullness and agitation is the skill developed here.

The fourth stage is called "immediate resting." As soon as a certain obstacle arises, we can either return to the object of meditation through the use of mindfulness or detect the obstacles of dullness and mental agitation whenever they occur. The level of distraction has decreased enormously. At this stage we no longer suffer from the second obstacle of forgetfulness—being unable to return to the object of meditation—and therefore the practice of mindfulness has more or less been mastered. Laziness is still present, however, as are the other obstacles, but gross forms of mental agitation do not arise.

The obstacles of dullness and mental agitation can manifest in both gross and subtle forms. Meditators who have reached the fourth stage have been able to overcome not only the obstacle of forgetfulness, but also a portion of the third obstacle, dullness and mental agitation. The dullness has not yet been handled, but a certain part of the agitation has been overcome, particularly in its more manifest aspects. There is an increasing necessity of relying on awareness to a greater degree, rather than mindfulness; we need to be more alert to detect the obstacle of dullness and mental agitation, since mindfulness has been mastered and forgetfulness does not cause a problem at this stage. Meditators must apply the antidote of awareness rigorously and need not be concerned about overapplication.

The fifth stage is known as "vigorous discipline." Since mindfulness has been achieved, there is a greater sense of ease, and the mind is not agitated or perturbed in an uncomfortable manner. Yet the literature on meditation says that this stage is very dangerous. Having been able to overcome a certain gross level of mental agitation, meditators may become complacent or suffer from plain boredom, with no emotions or thoughts to occupy the mind. Because there is no real agitation taking place, the meditators may be particularly vulnerable to the obstacle of dullness. Instead of being able to rest in a state of tranquillity with clarity, the mind may be robbed of clarity altogether. A sense of boredom and lack of interest may set in, while the obstacle of laziness has still not been overcome. At this stage one must pay particular attention to the obstacle of dullness, drowsiness, or stupor.

The sixth stage of tranquillity meditation is called "pacifying." Here meditators are able to deal not only with the gross level of mental agitation but also with the obstacles that originate from dullness, particularly in its gross form. Subtle forms of dullness have not yet been overcome, because this obstacle is generally harder to detect than that of mental agitation.

The seventh stage of shamatha is known as "thoroughly pacifying." At this level laziness may still arise from time to time, but it does not present major problems because conviction is so entrenched that we are not seduced by the different tendencies of laziness. Subtle forms of dullness and agitation may also still continue to occur at this stage. We must continue to be vigilant, lest we practice overapplication. Long-time meditators may continue to use antidotes out of habit, when in fact what they should be using is subtle forms of

awareness to overcome certain obstacles. Instead of applying awareness deliberately, for example, they should exercise awareness in a
gentle and more detached way. Meditators should practice equanimity and gradually try to break down the attitude of seeing the obstacles as being bad and the antidotes as being good. They should realize
that, through the practice of subtle forms of awareness, it is possible
to attain the state of tranquillity without exertion and without having
to consciously apply the relevant antidotes. For this reason the past
masters have suggested that here one should ease off and try to dwell
naturally in a state of tranquillity, rather than vigorously apply
antidotes.

The eighth stage is "one-pointedness." Now we have overcome
all the obstacles, even the fundamental one of mental dullness and
agitation, in both gross and subtle (or manifest and concealed) forms.
They do not need to apply awareness to remain in a state of tranquillity, because the obstacles no longer present any problems. This is
where a state of one-pointedness is achieved. Meditation has become
something natural, a way of being rather than something that has
to be created by warding off obstacles through the application of
antidotes.

The ninth and last stage is called "resting in equipoise," which is
more or less the culmination of shamatha practice and leads to the
complete mastery of pliancy of body and mind.

9

INSIGHT MEDITATION

The Paramita of Wisdom and the Madhyamaka School

THE SIXTH PARAMITA is concerned with insight meditation (*vipashyana*). Whereas the meditation of tranquillity is oriented toward stabilizing the mind, insight meditation is geared toward giving rise to insight or wisdom. When we practice tranquillity meditation, we are only interested in learning how to settle the mind and overcome distractions, in terms of the upsurge of thoughts and emotions. Insight meditation, on the other hand, makes use of thoughts and concepts. However, insight meditation has to be based upon the meditation of tranquillity.

According to Mahayana Buddhism, the sixth is the most important of all the paramitas, because without insight or wisdom, all the other paramitas remain on the mundane level, unable to assume spiritual significance. Paramitas such as generosity, patience, vigor, and even the practice of tranquillity meditation would be corrupted by our well-entrenched habits or deep-seated emotional conflicts and delusions. But it is possible to overcome these obstacles with the practice of insight meditation, so that our practice of the other paramitas can be real rather than provisional. The meditation of insight involves forms of reflection and contemplation, using thoughts and concepts, and with its cultivation we begin to understand more about ourselves and our relation to the external world and reality.

The practice of the other paramitas, which are oriented toward the development of compassion, is not sufficient for us to be able to achieve enlightenment; nor can we do so through the cultivation of wisdom alone. However, with the practice of insight meditation, all the paramitas can be integrated properly and enlightenment achieved. Wisdom and compassion must go hand in hand, as I have said before. This is a very important point. People often criticize Buddhists for being socially unaware. They say that we emphasize the idea of enlightenment, selflessness (or no-self), and meditation while neglecting the social aspects of day-to-day living. But the emphasis on compassion in Mahayana Buddhism means that our involvement with other human beings and other living creatures is just as important as spending time alone in quiet meditation.

Atisha says in *The Lamp of Enlightenment* (*Changchup Lamdön*): "Since insight without compassion, and compassion without insight, have been termed bondage, they must not be separated from each other." It is very important for us to spend time in meditation, trying to understand ourselves and our relationship with the world. At the same time, it is important for us to engage in various physical activities that will be beneficial for ourselves as well as others. In Mahayana Buddhism, compassion has a wider connotation than our normal understanding of that word. Here compassion involves being generous, tolerant, and understanding to all beings. It is not generated only toward people who are deprived of material goods or who are suffering from emotional afflictions.

The types of reflections practiced in insight meditation relate to what we call a meditative way of thinking. Rather than being speculative, it is a way of thinking that relates to practical life. This means that engaging in these kinds of reflections should have an immediate effect in terms of transforming us. It should transform our view of ourselves and the world. So even though insight meditation makes use of reasoning and logic, it does not deal only with abstract matters; it deals with real issues, with how we live and experience the world.

For this reason, in insight meditation we contemplate the question: What is the self? We also contemplate the relationship between the self and the external world, and the nature of ultimate reality. This sort of reflection is considered to be very important even if we have been meditating for a long time. If we have been practicing the meditation of tranquillity but have not been engaged in insight meditation, we will not be able to gain a real understanding of what is meant by the "self," or what our relationship with the world and ultimate reality is. If we do not have that understanding, then ignorance, the root cause of suffering, will never be eradicated.

MADHYAMAKA: THE SCHOOL OF THE MIDDLE WAY

Various aspects of Mahayana Buddhist philosophy are often used as the basis of insight meditation. There are two major schools of Mahayana Buddhism: one is Madhyamaka, the School of the Middle Way, and the other is called Yogachara or Chittamatra. We will start with Madhyamaka.

In the first chapter I touched on the idea of the Middle Way and how our understanding of ourselves, the nature of the world, and ultimate reality normally falls into the extremity of either eternalism or nihilism. As eternalists we believe that there is a permanent, unchanging, immutable self existing behind or beyond our bodies and our usual experiences of thoughts, feelings, emotions, and memories. In nihilism we think that there is no such thing as self, that there is no mind even, and that only the material world is real. In this materialist position, any concept of self or mind is reduced to brain processes or biological functions.

Different philosophies and religions posit the notion of an unchanging reality or Absolute. Some people understand this in a personal and theistic manner, while others understand it more in an impersonal and metaphysical way. But in both cases there is a belief in an unchanging, permanent, absolute reality that is substantial and inherently existing. Also, physical phenomena such as tables, chairs, mountains, houses, and people are seen as having an inherent existence and an enduring essence or substance. According to Mahayana Buddhism, this belief is founded on ignorance, and the notion of an enduring existence creates suffering. The Buddhist scholar Dignaga says: "When there is a self, one becomes conscious of the other. From 'I' and 'other' arises the belief in independent existence, and out of antagonism resulting from the union of these two, all evil comes about."

Out of our conflicting emotions, our sense of anxiety, our sense of uprootedness and alienation, comes this fundamental notion that there is a self that is locked up in our own body and completely independent from an external world. When these concepts are formed, all kinds of conflicting emotions arise, such as grasping, clinging, wanting certain possessions, aversion, hostility, and attempting to shun things that we want to avoid. From this, as Dignaga points out, come all kinds of evil and suffering. Madhyamaka philosophy uses the concept of emptiness as a therapeutic remedy for these ills of samsaric creatures. Realizing that no essences inhere in empirical objects diminishes our tendency to cling to things. Understanding emptiness allows us to see the world as it is and not believe the world as it appears to our deluded mind. Emptiness, or *shunyata*, in Madhyamaka philosophy does not mean that things do not exist. It does not mean that our everyday experience of the world is somehow completely erroneous, that it is all a dream. Many people in the West think this is exactly what the Mahayana tradition is saying. Just because things lack inherent existence or a permanent enduring essence does not mean they don't exist. Mountains, chairs, tables, houses, people, cars, and televisions all exist, but they do not have *inherent* existence.

How does this error arise? The error is not in thinking that things exist but in thinking that these things have some kind of substance that endures. We create problems in our lives precisely because we attach so much importance to things, thinking that they have enduring essence. Then we become so serious; we begin to cling, grasp, and can't let go. But if we can have the understanding that things do not have an enduring essence or substance, then we can become more flexible, less opinionated, and more accommodating. Emptiness means lack of inherent existence, or being empty of essence or substance.

Madhyamaka philosophy uses all kinds of reasoning to prove that things do not have an enduring essence. I will give just one example here, which relates to causality. Nagarjuna, the founder of Madhyamaka philosophy, says in his text known as *Mulamadhyamaka-karika* that "neither from itself nor from another, nor from both, nor without a cause, does anything whatever, anywhere arise." This means that things do not come into being because of a self-existing cause giving rise to a self-existing effect. If a thing came into being out of itself, completely independently of everything else, it should be able to give continuous rise to certain effects, but that does not happen. Things also do not arise from something other than themselves, another self-existing entity. If that were the case, there would be no causal relationship between the thing itself and the other. There has to be some kind of homogeneous relationship between cause and effect, which is unobtainable if we think of the thing itself and something else that gives rise to it as both being self-existing and totally independent of each other. Things cannot come into being due to both themselves and others, because this position would involve the defects of the previous two positions. If a thing comes into being through something other than itself, the whole idea of causality is put into jeopardy and everything becomes random; anything is able to give rise to anything else. As Nagarjuna said, this would lead to a complete breakdown of the whole idea of causality. Lastly, things do not come into being without any cause.

INTERDEPENDENT ORIGINATION
(*Pratitya-samutpada*)

How, then, do things come into being? They come into being because of what is called interdependent origination, or *pratitya-samutpada*— that is, due to causes and conditions. This implies that things do not have inherent existence, because if they had any kind of essence or independent existence there would be no need for the whole idea of causality. Nagarjuna says: "The origination of inherent existence from causes and conditions is illogical, since if inherent existence originated from causes and conditions, all things would thereby become contingent. How could there be contingent inherent existence? For inherent existence is not contingent; nor is it dependent on another being. So the very idea of causality involves the notion that things are contingent. There is no being that can exist on its own without depending on anything else; no self-sufficient being. Everything is interdependent. Everything that exists on both the physical and mental plane involves the idea of interdependence, or *pratitya-samutpada*."

The teachers of Mahayana Buddhism say that there are two things blocking or hindering us from appreciating this fact; the first obstacle is acquired and the other is innate. The acquired obstacle is that of education and cultural or religious accretions. I don't want to use the word *brainwashing*, although that immediately comes to mind. We have been inculcated in a particular way so that we do not stop to evaluate the truth of what we have absorbed through education and through certain familiar concepts. We fail to examine; we just accept things as fact whether they are true or not. These ideas may relate to either of the two extreme views of eternalism or nihilism.

The other obstacle is innate, which means that within the human condition there is an instinctive belief that things do have an enduring essence, even though these ideas are not formulated or articulated. It is said that the first obstacle is easier to deal with because, through intellectual understanding (of Madhyamaka philosophy, for example), we can get rid of a lot of these misconceptions. The innate obstacle is more difficult to overcome. Even when we know something intellectually, it is usually only through direct experience that we can gain understanding that fundamentally changes the way we think. For that reason we need to have immediate experience of emptiness. However, an intellectual understanding and direct experience are related through mediated understanding using concepts, reason, and so forth. Conceptual understanding can point us in the right direction; then we can have an intuitive or immediate understanding of emptiness.

Zen Buddhists use the example of pointing a finger at the moon. Concepts are useful as long as we don't look at the fingertip instead of the moon. The finger pointing at the moon can be useful because you know where to look. In a similar way, conceptual understanding should not be underestimated. Even though it does not deliver the final goods, so to speak, it is essential. Through conceptual understanding we gradually develop intuitive understanding, which dismantles the innate, instinctive belief in things having enduring essence, substance, or inherent existence.

EMPTINESS (*Shunyata*)

Through this type of analysis, the meditator comes to the realization that reality does not fall into either of the two extremes of eternalism or nihilism. Both the Buddha and Nagarjuna have said that the idea of interdependent origination is identical with the concept of emptiness. Nagarjuna has said that emptiness is interdependent origination and interdependent origination is emptiness. So when we say that things are interdependently produced, or that things come into being through the interdependence of causes and conditions, it is the same as saying things are empty by nature. Nagarjuna does not leave any doubt about this question; he says: "That which originates dependently we call emptiness. This apprehension is the understanding of the Middle Way. Since there is nothing whatsoever originating independently, nothing whatsoever exists that is not empty. So emptiness and interdependent origination mean the same thing, and that is the Middle Way."

Through the understanding of emptiness based upon interdependent origination, we are able to form the right view, which avoids these two extremes of eternalism and nihilism. In Madhyamaka philosophy, ultimate reality is not seen as something that exists outside of or above the empirical reality with which we are confronted every day. Rather, emptiness is the nature of the very world that we live in, so the nature of the empirical world is ultimate reality.

Normally a sharp contrast is made in philosophy and religion between the creation and the creator. There is a big gap between ultimate reality and empirical reality. This is true of the Western metaphysical system, in which the ultimate is atemporal, unchanging, and pure, while empirical reality is impure, changing, and imperfect. The view of the Middle Way is to posit a dialectical relationship between empirical reality and ultimate reality, wherein they cannot be separated. Ultimate reality is found in the midst of empirical reality and not somewhere else; nor is empirical reality denied or under-valued: this is the Middle Way.

Far from being a nihilistic idea, emptiness is in fact a very positive idea. It is because of emptiness that anything can exist at all in the first place. If things had an enduring essence or substance of some kind, we would have to have the concept of a static world. But the world is dynamic; it is not that emptiness causes things to come into being, but rather it allows them to come into being, just as space allows for things to be. Space is often used as an analogy for the concept of emptiness. If space is occupied by something, there is no room for something else to be there. It is because of space that any-thing and everything can come into being. In a similar way, emptiness allows things to come into existence. Without emptiness nothing could exist.

Because it is inconceivable to think of things not coming into existence, or existing eternally, Nagarjuna makes the following point in the *Mulamadhyamaka-karika*: "When shunyata is established, the whole world will be established. When shunyata is not realized, it is absurd to think that the whole world is real." Therefore, shunyata, instead of denigrating the world, affirms it; for it is thanks to empti-ness that the world exists, that we exist, and that there is such a thing as a spiritual path and a spiritual goal.

Another way of understanding the relationship between empiri-cal reality and ultimate reality, according to Madhyamaka philosophy, is through the notions of the two truths: relative or conventional truth, and absolute or ultimate truth. Relative truth refers to a per-ception of the empirical world as it exists. It can also include our distorted ways of apprehending this world, whereby we think of the world as having some kind of inherent existence. Ultimate truth re-fers to the perception of ultimate reality as emptiness, by means of intuitive understanding, insight, and wisdom.

Nagarjuna makes the point that it is through an understanding of relative truth that we can come to have some understanding of absolute truth. If we ignore or reject our experience of the world as it is, we can never gain any insight. As he says, ultimate truth will not be understood without being dependent upon relative truth. Again, with this concept of the two truths, we can see how they interrelate, and that ultimate truth is not something that exists independently of relative truth. In fact, the ultimate is understood only through an understanding of the relative, because ultimate truth is, in fact, the nature of relative truth. Only with this understanding can we establish the middle view, which is what the name of this particular school (Madhyamaka) means.

It is very important to realize that rejecting the inherent existence of things does not mean rejecting things as such—like houses, cars, and so forth. Nagarjuna repeatedly warns us against interpreting emptiness in such a way, and he is not the only one to do so. In other Mahayana sutras the same point has been made. In a text known as *Könchok Tsekpa* the Buddha says: "It is better to assume the existence of a real self, although this view is as big and obvious as Mount Meru.* Yet the pride of believing shunyata as a nonexistent entity is worse."

Even if one does not have a proper understanding of the lack of inherent existence of the self, and one assumes that there is an unchanging permanent self, Nagarjuna says that this is better than thinking that there is no self at all, or that everything is nonexistent. There is, after all, a practical everyday value in having a conventional notion of a self and the conventional existence of things and entities. The nihilistic view, on the other hand, is extremely dangerous, because it undermines all the ethical concerns of Buddhist theory and practice. Nagarjuna goes so far as to say that anyone who believes that things have an enduring essence or substance is as stupid as a cow, but to say that things have no existence at all is even more stupid (with all due respect to cattle).

Furthermore, the wise cling to neither existence nor nonexistence—that is the Middle Way. Those who have developed insight through reflection, contemplation, analysis, and meditation are able to rise above such notions. This is why wisdom is the most important of the six paramitas, because without it all the others have no meaning. Without it we would not have the understanding that the other paramitas lack inherent existence. So, too, with moral precepts or principles. Such an understanding can be gained only through the

*Mount Meru is the "world mountain" that stands at the center of the universe.

cultivation of insight, having a proper understanding of reality and the nature of the self.

This point is made clear by the Buddha in a sutra: "Even if one has kept the moral precepts for a long time and has practiced the meditation of tranquillity for millions of eons, when one does not properly understand the teaching of shunyata, no liberation is possible. He who knows the whole of reality to be lacking in inherent existence will never become attached to it."

That is the key: through understanding emptiness one is able to overcome attachment, clinging, and grasping. The Bodhisattva seeks to overcome attachment, not so as to become detached or indifferent to the world, but in order to get even more involved with the world. There is no longer that duality existing between the Bodhisattva and others—between the self and the world—because the self and the world both have the same nature, which is emptiness. Therefore, Bodhisattvas are able to execute their compassionate activities in a much more beneficial and far-ranging manner. As this particular sutra makes clear, even if we are doing the right thing according to moral principles, without wisdom we are not able to gain the full benefit from it.

IO

THE ROLE OF THE MIND

The Yogachara School and Buddha-Nature

THE OTHER SCHOOL of Mahayana philosophy is known as Yoga-chara. *Yoga* in this context means "meditation," while *chara* means "practice"; so *Yogachara* has been translated as "the school of meditation," emphasizing the primacy of meditation in understanding ulti-mate reality (not that the Madhyamaka school doesn't do this also).

This school is also called Chittamatra—a term that has given rise to much confusion in the West, where it has usually been translated as "mind only." This has led many interpreters of Mahayana Bud-dhism to think that this particular school denies the existence of the external world, positing that everything exists only in the mind. As a result, they consider Mahayana to be the same as the Western theory known as idealism. British idealists such as Bishop Berkeley assert that only ideas in the mind are real and that apart from ideas, nothing exists. This is not what the Chittamatrins mean when they say that everything is "mind only." What they mean is that our perception of external reality is mind-dependent. In other words, we can only have access to the external world through our mind.

Whereas the Madhyamikas emphasize the notion of emptiness, the Chittamatrins emphasize the mind. They say that through understanding how our perception of the external world is dependent upon the mind, we will be able to gain an understanding of emptiness.

THREE ASPECTS OF REALITY

The Chittamatrins or Yogacharins formulate three aspects of reality, called *svabhava* in Sanskrit. The first aspect of reality is *parakalpita svabhava*, which has been translated as the "notional-conceptual" level of reality. The Yogacharins say that when we look at things on all different levels—on the sensory level, the conceptual level, or the moral level—we can see that what we experience is colored by our presuppositions, prejudices, and predilections. This means that there is no such thing as objective reality in the ultimate sense.

On a sensory level, for example, we perceive a tree or car with our visual sense, but there is no tree or car existing of its own accord independently of the mind. Insects would not perceive a tree or a car in the way we would, because they lack our concepts relating to trees and cars. These are mental constructions imposed on the sensory impressions. In terms of concepts we can say that God exists or that God does not exist, but for either statement to be absolutely true there must be proof existing independently of the human mind. This also applies to ethics and morality. When people discuss issues like abortion, saying that it is always wrong, they are assuming that there is something absolutely true in itself, independent of the human mind. The Yogacharins say that there is no absolute truth in that sense. As we have seen, according to Madhyamaka philosophy, things lack an enduring essence and are empty of any inherent existence. Based upon this, the Yogacharins say that everything we experience is dependent upon the human mind.

The first of these three aspects of reality, then, is the notional-conceptual. The second aspect of reality is called the *paratantra svabhava*, which is generally translated as the "dependent" level of reality. This refers to the flow of mental phenomena within consciousness and the way in which we reify concepts, constructing the dualism of subject and object. The third and highest aspect of reality is called the *parinispanna svabhava*, or "ultimate reality." This level is devoid of any subject-object duality.

It is the dependent (paratantra) level of reality that is the most important level for the practitioner, because it is this level that connects ultimate reality with the notional-conceptual level of reality. Through meditation practice, we can undermine the dependent level by purifying it of its subject-object discriminations and thereby gain insight into the empty nature of this second aspect of reality. According to Yogachara, through practice and reflection the practitioner comes to realize that much of what we entertain on the notional-conceptual level has nothing to do with reality. This does not mean nothing exists at all, just that we experience it in a distorted manner.

For this reason, the paratantra principle is seen as the substratum—with a part that is deluded and a part that is not deluded—which is imbued with ultimate reality. Because the paratantra, or dependent level, acts as the basis for the parikalpita, or notional-conceptual level, it can be seen as the mediator between the notional-conceptual and the parinispanna, or ultimate level of reality.

We should not think that these three aspects of reality are completely different, since all are empty of nature, and it is only in relation to the deluded mind that we can talk about them at all. Although Yogacharin philosophers accept the notion of emptiness, they emphasize the important and creative role of the mind in how we experience and interact with the world. According to Yogachara philosophy, the source of our delusion is thinking that phenomena exist completely independently of the mind, and not seeing that things are in fact largely constructed by the mind itself.

DELUSION AND THE THREE LEVELS OF CONSCIOUSNESS

To explain how these delusions come about, Yogachara philosophy is unique in positing three levels of consciousness: ordinary consciousness (*vijnana*), which consists of the five sense consciousnesses plus the thinking mind with all its thoughts, feelings, impressions, and images; the egocentric mind (*manas*); and the substratum of consciousness (*alayavijnana*), often called the storehouse consciousness.

Delusions arise from the interaction of these three levels of consciousness. Whatever we experience about the world through our senses is relayed through the egocentric mind. The resultant distorted information is then retained on the substratum of consciousness, the alayavijnana, which has sometimes been compared to the Western notion of the unconscious. According to Yogachara, this is how karmic imprints become entrenched in the mind, and these arise later to influence the way we perceive the world through our senses. Owing to the interaction of these three levels of consciousness, reality becomes distorted. In other words, we have access only to the first aspect of the reality, the notional-conceptual, and have no idea about the relative or the ideally absolute.

The mindfulness and awareness of meditation practice enable us to see how this interaction takes place, how the senses are influenced by these karmic imprints, which arise involuntarily, and how we are often not aware of this process. At the same time, we see how our perception of the external world leaves imprints on our mind, thus fueling the fire of our habitual patterns. The less aware we are, the more habituated we become, and the more we become victimized by the alayavijnana.

The aim of meditation is to transform the alayavijnana. When a fundamental change takes place on this storehouse level, we begin to see how deceived we have been in thinking that things have some kind of independent existence. We do not realize that what we normally consider to be the external world is largely constructed by the mind itself. We can see the deceptive nature of the first aspect of reality—the notional-conceptual—and we begin to gain some appreciation of the two other aspects, the dependent principle and the ideally absolute or ultimate reality.

BUDDHA-NATURE

Another contribution that the Yogachara school has made to the general Mahayana tradition and philosophy is the notion of Buddha-nature or *tathagatha-garbha* (Tibetan, *teshek nyingpo*). Many people in the West have heard about this Mahayana concept, which is only associated with Yogachara philosophy. Madhyamaka philosophers talk about absolute and relative bodhichitta, but they do not talk about Buddha-nature as such. Relying on certain authoritative Mahayana sutras, the Yogacharins formulated this concept, by saying that all sentient beings have the seed or potential to obtain enlightenment. No one is excluded. Even if people are not aware of it now, they may become aware of it in the future. It is quite interesting to consider that if everybody has Buddha-nature, then so too must Christians, Jews, Muslims, and Hindus. If, then, they can all become enlightened, does that mean that they must eventually become Buddhists? This raises many interesting questions that I am not going to dwell on at this time; it is a very contentious issue nonetheless. Yogacharins say that all beings—not just human beings, but all sentient beings—have the capacity to become enlightened. Although some will attain enlightenment sooner than others, everyone will achieve enlightenment eventually.

This concept of Buddha-nature has been interpreted in different ways. Some say that everyone has the potential to attain perfection but do not consider human beings as having a perfect nature. Others have interpreted Buddha-nature to mean that not only do people possess Buddha-nature, but this nature is already perfect and complete. The only difficulty is that we do not realize it! It is not like a seed that, left to develop, gives rise to a plant or sprout. Our Buddha-nature is already fully formed or developed, and only the adventitious defilements stand between us and enlightenment. These defilements simply need to be removed through practice.

When we embark on the spiritual journey, we have to realize that we do have the capacity to realize our goals. If we did not have that capacity, then spiritual realization would only be a dream. It would be like a person without arms imagining that he was picking up a huge piece of rock. He can imagine it but he does not have the capacity, I am sorry to say. If people do not have the capacity to see, then you cannot tell them to look. The point is, when we are expected to do something and do it well, we have to have the capacity for it to begin with. Therefore, Buddha-nature represents that spiritual capacity that we already have within ourselves.

Now, if we were innately or intrinsically evil, confused, or deluded, where would that capacity to overcome our delusions come from? We have to have the capacity to transcend our delusions, to go beyond our confusions, to go beyond the various psychological pollutants of the mind. We do have that capacity, according to Mahayana teachings. However, capacity and ability are not the same. We have the capacity, but we may not have the ability. How so? One may have certain talents to do a certain thing, perhaps to play music, paint, write poetry, or some innate talent for philosophizing. Nevertheless, to have ability, we must do something with the capacity that we have. That depends upon a variety of factors, such as the company that we keep, the situations that we are in, and the general opportunity to develop and cultivate our innate capacity. If you have a container full of wheat or barley then you have potential seeds. If you put them into the soil, they have the potential to grow and sprout. However, if you do not do that, then those grains do not have the ability to flourish. They have the capacity, the potentiality to sprout, but they need nourishment to do so. There has to be proper soil. You cannot just take some grains and plant them on the beach. That will not work, the soil condition has to be right. Then you have to water it, and the conducive climactic conditions have to be there. So when we talk about Buddha-nature, the situation is no different. Why? Because while we already have the capacity to attain enlightenment, not all human beings are the same. We have to aim toward equality, we have to aspire toward equality but we are not equal. In fact, we are very different.

FIVE FAMILIES

According to the Mahayana teachings, there are many different kinds of people in the world, but in terms of the spiritual path there are five fundamental categories of people. In texts dealing with Buddha-nature, these different spiritual types are referred to as five families.

The first one is called *rik che*. *Rik* means "family," and *che* means "cut off," therefore "cut-off family." Now what does that mean? It means that despite having the capacity to attain enlightenment, the members of this family, because of various circumstances and situations, including inner psychological inhibitions and resistances, may not avail themselves of that opportunity of awakening. For example, someone brought up in a very violent society or family and taught nothing but violence would not be likely to pay any attention to his or her need to grow spiritually. In this case, the person has the capacity but not the ability. So that is the cut-off family.

The second type is called *ma nge*. *Ma* means "uncertain" or "ambiguous," and *nge* is "family." Individuals belonging to this "ambiguous family" do have the interest, but it depends very much on what opportunities are available, what sort of people they come into contact with, what spiritual teachings they receive, and then what they choose to do with those opportunities. Their situation is open. Therefore, *ma nge* can go one way or the other. In the first group, there was very little chance that an individual would even bother about going to a church, let alone come to a Buddhist retreat center. This person can go either way; that's why it's called the "indeterminate" or "ambiguous" family.

The next spiritual type is the Shravaka, or *nyenthö*. *Nyen* means people who listen to spiritual teachings, who have some sort of interest or inclination, who want to know more about spiritual teachings and practices. However, they do not in fact do any real practice themselves. It is more a question of accumulating knowledge; they want to know what the teacher said, who lived when, who said what to whom. There is obviously great curiosity about spiritual matters, but no real practice. Some Mahayanists think of Shravakas as being the same as Theravadins, which is totally mistaken. The Theravadins are not equated with the concept of Shravakas. It should be pointed out that Buddhism has always encouraged scholarship and the pursuit of all kinds of artistic endeavors. In fact, many of the Buddhist masters were great poets, great scholars, great artists or sculptors. The point is that if that is all that one is doing—if one is only thinking, "I have to accumulate knowledge, I have to just learn and learn and learn," without actually putting it into practice—then one remains on the level of the Shravaka, or the hearer family.

The fourth family is known as Pratyekabuddha, or *rang sanggye*. The Tibetan term means attaining realization through one's own efforts. *Rang* means "through one's own method," and *sanggye* means "realization." Individuals belonging to this family have understood the importance of spiritual practice. They may have already accumulated enough knowledge, and now they want to practice. However, they do not want to practice with other people, they want to do it on their own. They are individualists who do not conform to any particular lineage, tradition, or system. They are people who want to dissent and secede, and who may in fact be branded as heretical. This family is about applying oneself vigorously without wanting to have anything to do with a particular religious tradition. It is said that the Pratyekabuddha realizes that everything is impermanent by contemplating the principle of interdependent origination (*pratitya-samutpada*). For example, when you see someone who has died, you contemplate death and realize that it has come from birth. Through seeing that everything is causally conditioned, you can conclude that everything is impermanent and can gain some kind of spiritual realization in that way.

The fifth spiritual type is the Bodhisattva (*changchup kyi sempa*). *Changchup* means "awakening," and *sempa* means "being." These individuals have not only realized the importance of practice but actually want to do something about their practice in relation to others. For them practice is not an individual preoccupation, because they are not doing it only for their own benefit. They are not thinking, "I have to do something because I can understand that my life has become a mess, and I have to get myself out of this predicament." One can go further than this and say, "I want to practice and I want to help other people, through my practice, through the development of love and compassion." That is the Bodhisattva family.

So we have got the cut-off type, the ambiguous type, and the type who have embarked on the path with a more intellectual than practice-oriented interest. Then there is the type who only practice for their own benefit, and finally the individuals who are motivated by the interests of others as well as their own. This last type is considered the best in terms of how to realize our inner condition. In this way, we can see that we all have the capacity to become enlightened. However, our ability to realize that potential varies from individual to individual. We all have the same capacity, but some individuals are closer than others to their own natural state, which is Buddha-nature.

THE IDEA OF THE HOLY

Religious philosophers and sociologists all seem to agree on one thing. In all the major world religions, such as Christianity, Buddhism, Hinduism, Judaism, Islam, and the tribal religions (what used to be known as primitive religions), the main spiritual focus revolves around the idea of the holy. There has to be something sacred, something holy. It does not matter whether you are living in the Amazonian jungles of Brazil, running around barefoot in central Australia, or riding a yak in the mountains of Tibet. All of these different people share a similar religious focus, and that is the need to see something as being holy. Everyday experience is not what leads us to find real fulfillment; rather, fulfillment comes about through contemplating something other than the empirical world in which we live. We find our salvation through contemplating something that is sacred, because we do not think that what we are already experiencing is sacred.

A German theologian named Rudolf Otto, who wrote the books *Idea of the Holy* and *Mysticism, East and West,* says that the idea of the holy has a compelling attraction, like a magnet. At the same time, what is considered holy can also generate an enormous sense of trepidation and fear as well as hope. He called this feeling *mysterium tremendum. Mysterium* means that what is holy is transcendent, beyond our grasp. Its power comes from the fact that we cannot fully comprehend it because of the limited capacity we have as human beings to grasp things that are not normal. It is *tremendum* because whatever is the "other," whatever is transcendent, is seen as being a source of dread and fear.

Ancient religions related to gods in a way that allowed for a real sense of closeness between the individual and the gods that they worshiped. They worshipped the gods because they were helpful, but they also feared them at the same time. That is not different from the early Greeks and Romans. Whatever is holy, whatever is godly or divine, is seen as being both attractive and fearful. It is the same with the God of Judaism and Christianity.

According to Western religious scholars, then, the source of religion lies in this human tendency to be attracted to something other than ourselves, but at the same time to experience dread, fear, and awe in relation to it. In most of the world's religions, except for within certain mystical teachings, the source of what we perceive to be sacred comes from somewhere else, a transcendental source. According to Buddhism, however, the source of holiness is within ourselves. Therefore, it is through practice that we realize that there is a spiritual spring, a reservoir of good, within ourselves. That is what the Mahayana teachings say.

The concept of Buddha-nature is about this inherent holiness. We do not have to be injected with something or receive something from outside as a gift. We do not have to accept any gifts, because we already have what it takes to go where we want to go. In that sense—to put it theologically or philosophically—we can say that what is immanent and what is transcendent have come together. Buddha-nature is transcendent, in the sense that it is not contained by our ego identity. We have to rise above that everyday experience of who we believe we are. On the other hand, Buddha-nature is not something that exists outside of our body and mind, our mental and physical conditions. Therefore, it is both immanent and transcendent.

In any case, Rudolf Otto may be right in saying that we have a very ambiguous approach to our spiritual experiences. We have that in relation to our Buddha-nature as well. For example, people sometimes say that when they meditate, they have experiences that scare them because they do not know where they are going. The experience of going into uncharted territory evokes a sense of fear and dread, even awe. Yet where we are going is no different from where we already are. It's not as if we are stepping outside of our physical and mental condition and becoming united with an entity outside ourselves. In realizing Buddha-nature, we are taking a journey in which we will return home and find our own "original dwelling place." This is the expression used in certain teachings of both Tibetan and Zen Buddhism, the original dwelling place. Buddha-nature is the original dwelling place.

We might use the term *Buddha-nature* or *tathagatagarbha* as an abstract concept, but in fact, it is not. It is that place where we find ourselves when we are meditating; it is always there. In that way,

Buddha-nature is both transcendent and immanent. The soteriological or salvific import of the concept of Buddha-nature lies in the fact that the contemplative attempt to develop an understanding of Buddha-nature allows us to understand who we are. Normally we try to understand who we are in relation to our ego identity, our ego concept. To try to think about ourselves in relation to our Buddha-nature is to think of ourselves from a different perspective, with a wide-angle lens, as it were.

QUALITIES OF BUDDHA-NATURE

According to our definition, to have Buddha-nature is to have the capacity to become enlightened; yet this does not necessarily mean that we have the ability or the means to attain enlightenment. To realize Buddha-nature we have to have a sense of confidence that enlightenment is not some kind of distant possibility but something that we can achieve and experience presently. We may think of enlightenment as existing somewhere in the distance, at the terminus point of our journey. In such a scenario, there is initially no enlightenment and no enlightening experience that one can have. However, that is not the case; enlightenment does not occur only at the end of our journey. It is not as if we have disembarked from this rickety samsaric railway carriage and suddenly go, "Wow, this is real paradise here after all." It is not like taking those rough train journeys in India where arriving at your destination is the cause of relief! In fact, enlightening experiences occur all the time when you meditate. That is what the concept of Buddha-nature represents.

The teachings on Buddha-nature emphasize that enlightened qualities are already present in us. It is not that we are unredeemable wretched creatures who then develop certain qualities and become enlightened beings blazing with insight, wisdom and wit. What these teachings are saying is that the enlightened qualities are already there. So we need to understand that enlightenment is not a state but a process. We should not be thinking about Buddha-nature as some kind of fixed state, because Buddha-nature and our enlightening experiences go hand in hand. If Buddha-nature were a fixed state, it would have nothing to do with the dynamic process of approaching enlightenment or becoming more enlightened.

Enlightenment and delusion are not two radically different and independent states of being. Rather, delusions and the enlightened experience are interdependent. When you look at it like that, you realize that the experiences and the indications that we receive from having Buddha-nature are not so remote, not so inaccessible and out of reach. They are immediate. In fact, Buddha-nature is our aboriginal state. If it is aboriginal, or primordial, it must be intrinsic to our nature, and if it is intrinsic to our nature, how can we be so distant from it?

In traditional Mahayana literature our samsaric condition is described as impure, permeated with suffering, impermanent, and lacking in self. In the tathagatagarbha literature, however, Buddha-nature is said to be pure, while only samsara is said to be impure—it is pervaded by suffering and impermanent. Self, therefore, is a contingent phenomenon. In the *Mahayanuttara-tantra-shastra*, which is entirely devoted to a description of Buddha-nature, it is said that Buddha-nature has the qualities of purity, bliss, permanency, and great self. When we look at the concept of Buddha-nature, then, we see that the whole domain of our experience has been revised. Instead of suffering, there is bliss; instead of impermanence, there is a sense of permanence, and so forth.

Purity

As you can imagine, concepts like these have generated quite a bit of controversy. What does it mean to be pure, and what does it mean to be impure? Again, according to the *Mahayanuttaratantra*, we can understand purity and impurity in two different ways. First, we can understand purity in relation to Buddha-nature itself. Buddha-nature has intrinsic purity (*rangshin namdak*) like a crystal or mirror. However, although the mirror itself is pure, it can get dust on it. For example, an old mirror that has been languishing in the attic will be covered with dust and cobwebs. You cannot see anything. However, if you wipe that mirror clean, then it has the capacity to reflect. In other words, just because Buddha-nature is intrinsically pure, this does not mean we will necessarily have any experience of that purity. We have to engage in practices of all kinds—all the basic dusting, washing, and wiping necessary to bring the mirror back to its original condition. So this is called temporal purity (*lobur trel dak*) because now the adventitious defilements have been removed from the mind as well.

Bliss

The second quality that Buddha-nature possesses is bliss (*dewa*). Buddha-nature is bliss precisely because when we are not interacting with the world from an egocentric viewpoint, we are coming from a point that is open and receptive. We are responding to things rather than reacting to them. When we operate under the influence of ego, with its selfishness, arrogance, self-centeredness, neediness, and greed, we become so completely one-directional and fixated that our vision becomes extremely narrowed. Therefore there is no bliss, only more trials and tribulations from which we can only expect more anxiety, fear and insecurity. The fear of not being liked, of not being accepted—all these things come to the surface and take over. But when one begins to have some intimation of the original state of Buddha-nature through meditation practice, then there is bliss.

Finally we realize how it is possible to become confident without having to be arrogant, selfish, or self-centered, always thinking that we have to come first before anything or anybody else. When our ego identity is so strong we do not feel connected to other people, we do not feel connected to anything. Consequently, our relationship to other people and the world generally suffers. When we are like that, when we have a strong ego identity and we become self-absorbed, we may think, "I'm looking after myself, I *have* to look after myself." However, we are not really doing that at all, according to these teachings. In fact, we are doing the opposite. We are really on a suicide mission in a way, because the more self-absorbed and selfish we become, the more difficult it will be for other people to relate to us. We become a nuisance to others and a nuisance to ourselves as well. There is no bliss then; only more pain is in store.

When we practice, and when we become more in touch with our

true condition—which is the Buddha-nature—there is a greater sense of relaxation, a greater sense of openness and receptiveness. This provides the conditions for us to be able to respond to things more appropriately and act in a way that is helpful for both others and ourselves, because what is external and what is internal are not different. Then there is bliss.

Permanence

The third quality of Buddha-nature is permanence (*takpa*). Here we have to be very careful, for this does not mean permanency in the sense of something that is static, but permanency in the sense of not being swayed by whimsical moods. On a good day, you go to a Buddhist temple, meet this great master, and receive his blessing. You have a fantastic audience, the rapport is there, and everything is hunky-dory. You feel uplifted, your mood is good and you're feeling all energized and optimistic. Then you come out of the temple and realize that you have a parking ticket, and you're as mad as hell. All that upliftedness is gone in a second. The feeling of greatness and sense of connectedness that you felt with the teacher has disappeared in a flash. The permanency of Buddha-nature is not like that. It is permanency in the sense that our mood swings and ups and downs in life do not affect the quality of our enlightened state. Our mind might be swayed this way and that way, pushed and pulled and disturbed. But whatever is happening in the mind does not affect our enlightened state. That is why the quality of permanency cannot be understood in the sense of being some kind of static state. The Buddha-nature is not a state at all.

Great Self

"Great self" (*dak*) refers to the fact that we all have to be somebody. No one wants to become nobody. We all want to improve our lives; we all want to have a more enriching, happy life. None of us wants to end up not amounting to anything, or thinking that we didn't do anything to improve our life, or made absolutely nil contribution to the welfare of the society in which we live. Therefore, the notion of the self is very strong and very important in terms of how we see ourselves, how we treat other people and ourselves, how we view things. All of these things relate back to the self. Even to wish for and aspire toward enlightenment requires the concept of the self. We cannot do it otherwise. If there is no one in the train, then the train is empty. We may want to go to Venice or Florence, but we cannot just imagine that we are there. We have to board the train; we have to hand in our ticket. The spiritual path also requires that someone has taken the journey. Otherwise who is going to benefit from practicing, who is going to get anything out of it? If practice means dismantling all notions of one's self, then whatever this concept of self is could totally disintegrate. Then it would have been a very tedious, painful, and ultimately self-defeating task—a journey that has led to an abyss; a train that has gone off the edge of the cliff.

I think it is very important to understand that practice does not mean we get rid of the notion of ourselves altogether. We have to understand that the self-image we have is a construction of the mind. It has its use, albeit a limited use. Through practice we have to rise above it and go beyond it, all the while relating to that conventional self—the ordinary everyday self. We have to refer constantly to this conventional self, but we also have to go beyond it. As I said previously, in terms of transcendence, we have to step out of the conventional ideas of who and what we are; otherwise the tendency to perpetuate our old well-entrenched habits will continue forever. With the concept of Buddha-nature, we have a greater sense of self—great self—not the self that we are accustomed to, but a self where we are able to rise above that conventional self. We can relate more clearly, observe more, become more sensitive, have more feelings of connection.

How Buddha-Nature Exists

Buddha-nature has those four characteristics, but what is the status of Buddha-nature? To put it in philosophical terms, what is the ontological status of Buddha-nature apart from its soteriological orientation and salvific import? In terms of its ontological status, our mind is constantly bogged down by thoughts of whether something exists or does not exist. If something exists it is real; if something does not exist, it is not real. This dualistic way of thinking is so predominant and so much a part of our mental habit that we find it very difficult to escape from. However, when we start to think about the ontological status of Buddha-nature, we do not think about existence and nonexistence. Buddha-nature does not exist in the same way as tables and chairs. Nevertheless, it is also not nonexistent. The ontological status of Buddha-nature—how the Buddha-nature exists—is different from how everything else exists. We cannot say Buddha-nature exists in the way we think of empirical objects in the world existing, or even mental states. When we say everyone is in the possession of Buddha-nature it is not like owning something. It is not like owning a house or a car or a body. We think it should be like this; we have a house, we have furniture—that's the way it should be, that's the kind of world we should be living in—but we don't own Buddha-nature in that way. The closest analogy for Buddha-nature is that of space. Space does not exist as the clouds within space exist; the way it exists is of a different order. We cannot say whether space exists, meaning we cannot say it is like some substantial, inherently existing thing, and we cannot say that it does not exist, that it's nothing. Space is not nothing because without space—again to a Buddhist way of reasoning—we would not have all the galaxies and planets; even this thought would not be here.

In a fashion, Buddha-nature exists, but to say that it exists is more like a metaphor. You can only really refer to it in an oblique fashion; you cannot pin it down so easily, because Buddha-nature in itself is nothing; it is not a substance. Buddha-nature is not a psychic substance of any kind. It is intrinsically empty, but at the same time, Buddha-nature is the source of enlightenment. Without Buddha-nature, we would not be able to attain enlightenment. If there were only ignorance, conflicting emotions and conceptual proliferation, it would be impossible to find a way out. So in that sense, Buddha-nature exists, but it does not exist as a substantial entity.

According to Mahayana Buddhism, Buddha-nature is not part of causes and conditions, but is self-presenting. We develop a whole new perspective in relation to how we see ourselves when we no longer operate from within the conventional context of ego identity. We have a more expansive view in relation to our abilities and how we are able to see things. We are less opinionated; one is able to embrace things more. That in itself becomes a liberating force. To be somebody, to have a rich life, to have a life-affirming attitude, does not require one to be self-centered, greedy, or dependent. In fact, when we begin to learn how to rise above our self-image, our life becomes automatically enriched—spiritually, psychologically, in relationships, and in all kinds of other ways. Ego obsession is imprisoning; we become so self-absorbed that we are totally closed off, oblivious to our surroundings and to other people. All we can think of is our own pain, unhappiness, and frustration. That is why samsara is painful. If, through meditation practice, we can make a little more sense of what it is to be in our original dwelling place—the Buddha-nature—then we come home. We feel a sense of connectedness, less alienated, less cut off. It is not always the case that other people are alienating us; we do that to ourselves. Each individual is communicating less and less and then we start to wonder, "Why isn't anyone talking to me? Why is that person acting in such a manner?" Is it because we have become so self-absorbed that we are thinking that everyone has turned against us? In fact, it may even be the other way around: there may be people trying to communicate and trying to help, but because of self-absorption, we cannot see it, we have become totally closed off. So there is no feeling of connectedness. That is why it is so important to have some understanding of Buddha-nature.

II

SPIRITUAL PROGRESS

The Five Paths and the Ten Stages
of the Bodhisattva

THE CONCEPT OF "PATH" is extremely important in Buddhism, which places emphasis on our individual capacity to achieve liberation or enlightenment by ourselves, rather than relying on the power of another. When we embark on a journey, when we travel on the path, we must do so alone. No one else can do it on our behalf. It is like getting to know a new country: if we want to see it, we must go there ourselves. Others may come back with photographs and give us an idea of what the place is like, but this is no substitute for our firsthand experience.

However, people who have visited a particular place and come back with photos and stories may be able to tell us how to actually make that journey ourselves, and how to make it in a pleasant rather than a painful way. In a similar way, even though we must make the spiritual journey ourselves, we can receive guidance and information from others, and this is provided by Buddhas and Bodhisattvas. In this way, from the Buddhist perspective, embarking on the spiritual journey, or traveling on the path, is an essential concept.

The other notion involved with this idea of traveling on the path is that even if there is no substantial, permanent, independent, inherently existing self or ego, that does not mean that there is no one to travel on the path, that there is no one to become transformed from a state of delusion and confusion.

Egolessness is not the same as self-extinction. We do not cease to exist, but we come to know more about ourselves. Realizing that there is no unchanging self can in fact be an enriching experience. The path consists of working with ourselves so that gradually, by overcoming the various inhibitions, confusions, and delusions of the mind, we start to develop more insight into our own nature.

When we look at ourselves in the present moment, we see all kinds of confusions and defilements in our mind. Yet the possibility of overcoming all that and becoming enlightened is a reality. Our own lives become enriched from having undertaken this journey. So it's important not to mistranslate this concept of selflessness or nonexistence of ego. To say that we do not exist at all is the nihilistic view, which the Buddha rejected completely.

As we saw earlier, there are two different ways to attain the goals of liberation and enlightenment. One is the Shravaka method, which aims to attain enlightenment for one's own sake. The other is the Bodhisattva approach, which consists in working for the benefit of others and thereby attaining enlightenment. Both approaches are legitimate. We can attain the goal from either perspective. Whichever approach we take, there are five stages of progress or development along the path that we travel: the path of preparation (also called the path of accumulation), the path of application, the path of seeing, the path of meditation, and the path of no more learning. The first two, the path of preparation and the path of application, are normally referred to as worldly paths, whereas the last three are known as supramundane paths. On the last three paths, there is a greater development of wisdom. From the Buddhist perspective, without wisdom we operate on the level of a worldly person. No matter how kindhearted we are, or how well behaved we may be, if we are devoid of wisdom, we are still operating within the context of this world and not the world of spirituality.

Wisdom does not necessarily mean being clever. Wisdom in Buddhism has more to do with having a real understanding of ourselves and the phenomenal world. On the Shravaka level it means understanding impermanence, and on the level of the Bodhisattva it means understanding emptiness. A really spiritual person must possess the qualities of compassion and love as well as wisdom. Even if compassion and love are present in the mind-stream of a particular individual, if that person is lacking in wisdom he or she is still not a fully developed person.

THE PATH OF PREPARATION

On the path of preparation or accumulation, we must initially recognize that the samsaric condition in which we have been living is completely unsatisfactory and unfulfilling. Without that recognition, there is absolutely no chance of making any kind of spiritual progress at all. The samsaric condition is basically a condition of the mind, not of the external world (although many people assume otherwise). Samsara is not the material world in which we live—houses, trees, mountains, rivers, animals, and so forth; rather, it is the mind that is constantly busy and never able to remain still for a moment. The samsaric condition is created by a mind that constantly reaches out, grasping this and rejecting that, filled with immense craving, which a person will do anything to satisfy. Much of the time, the delusion of anger or hostility has its origins in this first delusion of excessive desire. When excessive desire is present, anger and hostility naturally arise because they are evoked by frustrated desires.

What produces this agitation of the mind, itself caused by excessive desire or hostility and resentment, is the presence of ignorance. This means not realizing what is really beneficial for ourselves and what is really harmful. If we are able to realize that the negative emotions in which we indulge are not at all helpful but are in fact extremely harmful, the desire to overcome them will arise.

We must come to this realization because we are seeking true, lasting, permanent happiness. We normally think that this kind of happiness can be obtained by grasping at things that by their own nature are impermanent. So we think, for example, that if we get married, all of our problems will be solved; if we have children, that will be wonderful; if we get a promotion at work, many of our problems will disappear. Buddhism does not say that we ought not to have experiences of temporal happiness or pleasure. But it does say that we do not normally think of these as temporal pleasures; in fact, we think of them as a permanent source of happiness, and this is where our mistake lies, caused by our ignorance.

Naturally this does not mean that we should necessarily reject experiences of temporal happiness or pleasure, but we should realize that these are only temporary, because whatever we can obtain in this life can also be lost. Children can be lost, we can be divorced from our spouses, we can lose our jobs, we can suffer loss in terms of business—all these things can and do happen. If we have not followed a spiritual path, our life will be completely devastated by such events, because we have concentrated purely on what we have rather than what we are.

Spiritual practice is about being, or becoming, a different person; having a different experience of our own being. It has scarcely anything to do with what we have in terms of job, family, and so forth. This does not mean that we should reject our family in order to be spiritual, or that we should stop working and live in the jungle in order to be spiritual. Even the happiness that we may feel in the jungle will turn into unhappiness when the mosquitoes and the snakes start biting! Real happiness has to come from within, from having a greater understanding of ourselves. As our inner struggles and conflicts gradually lessen and we become more integrated, we gain a sense of peace. We will not stop having problems in life, because many problems come from the external world. However, the inner sense of integration enables us to deal with whatever arises in our life. This is the kind of thing we have to work with on the path of preparation.

We begin to realize where the real source of happiness lies, and this makes us keen to pursue the path. If we are not convinced, if we are not looking forward to our destination, the journey cannot take place.

The Four Foundations of Mindfulness

We now turn to some of the subjects and practices described in previous chapters, and place them in the context of the Mahayana path.

The path of preparation is divided into three stages. At the first stage, the practitioner has to realize that meditation is the antidote for the fragmented, distorted, and confused mind that experiences inner conflicts. No other method is more efficient than the practice of meditation, which enables different kinds of centering of the self to take place. This is different from ego-centeredness or self-centeredness. It is achieved through shamatha, the meditation of tranquillity, which has to be complemented by the practice of vipashyana, the meditation of insight. In this particular case, the vipashyana practice consists of the four foundations of mindfulness. The four foundations of mindfulness are mindfulness of body, mindfulness of feeling, mindfulness of mind, and mindfulness of the phenomenal world. Through the practice of vipashyana the meditator comes to realize that everything is subject to change. From the Buddhist point of view the understanding of impermanence is fundamental. Some people understand this on an intellectual level only, but it has to become a personal experience. If the way in which we live our life reflects this understanding, rather than a mere intellectual knowledge of it, when changes occur in our life we are actively helped by this understanding.

In order to personalize this understanding, we engage in the practice of the four foundations of mindfulness. What could be more personal than our own body, feeling, and mind, and our own perception of the phenomenal world through the senses? We observe the body to see changes on the physical level; we observe our feelings of joy, pain, and so on; and we observe our mind—its thoughts, concepts, whatever is arising in it. For example, we may think we are depressed, and this seems to be one continuous state of mind. But as we become more observant of the mind, we realize that even our depressed state is interrupted by moments of joy, or of some other state.

Similarly, we also realize that what we perceive through our senses of the external world is subject to change. In the material world, some changes occur very rapidly, while others occur only very slowly but at a steady pace. Geologists say the Himalayas are becoming taller, but this is happening so slowly that we cannot observe it. Nonetheless it is taking place. So even those material things that seem very solid and real are also insubstantial, in the sense that they are also subject to change. They are not immobile or static. On the level of the first path, the path of preparation, the practitioner has some real understanding of impermanence, which is gaining insight into the nature of things. This is different from the shamatha experience of tranquillity.

This experience of impermanence should be seen as a positive rather than a negative. We should not despair because everything perishes. To be vibrant, to be active, not to remain in a state of inertia, is a good thing. Change in all different ways can be a very positive experience. If there were no change, how could we ever overcome our delusions? How would it be possible to eradicate ignorance and defilements? It's possible precisely because mind and consciousness can be transformed by practice and training. The whole idea of transformation means change. That's how an ordinary sentient being can become an Arhat or Buddha.

The Four Abandonments

The second stage of the path of preparation is attained when the individual starts to progress in the practice of the four abandonments. These four practices consist of trying to exercise control over our negativities and at the same time trying to prevent potential negativities from arising in the future. Buddhism asserts that there is an intimate relationship between thoughts and actions, and there is thus a connection between the practice of morality and our sense of well-being and health. The practice of morality is not just a matter of following rules, acting out of a sense of duty and obligation. We engage in wholesome deeds precisely because this is how we can experience a positive state of mind. This in turn leads us to the experience of physical and mental well-being. Conversely, engaging in negative states of mind leads us to behave negatively. This produces further mental agitation, anxiety, and fear, which cause imbalance in both mind and body.

Being positive in this context means that we are observant in the practice of mindfulness, observing our body, speech, and mind. It is said that negative habits are formed through not paying enough attention to our physical behavior and our verbal and mental processes. So we need to become more attentive. This is not the same as being self-conscious. Sometimes people say that they have been trying to practice mindfulness but that causes them to become self-conscious, and when they become self-conscious they feel paranoid. It's not as if we are observing ourselves in the same way that someone else would watch us. That would just make us feel exposed and very vulnerable. We simply look at what's going on in our mind and how we operate in the world.

Modern neurologists and other scientists also say that our character and personality are intimately linked to our sense of well-being, and the likelihood of our suffering from heart disease, high blood pressure, and similar conditions. Since Buddhists view thoughts, emotions, actions, morality, and physical and mental well-being as interconnected, we engage in these four contemplations: first, preventing potential negativities from arising; second, trying to deal with those which have already arisen; third, cultivating positive qualities that have not yet arisen; and last, developing those which have already arisen.

It's important to realize that our negative thoughts and emotions are not negative in an absolute form, but only in relation to the effects they have on our mind and our state of being. That's why they should be avoided, not because they are inherently bad. So when they arise, we should just think of them as negativities with which we have to work and which can be overcome.

The Four Limbs of Supernatural Powers

The last stage of the path of preparation is achieved when the practitioner applies what are called the four limbs of supernatural powers. Here the miracle has more to do with hard work than any kind of intervention from the divine. The first limb is inclination, the second is effort, the third is intention, and the last is analysis.

First of all, we must have the inclination, or we would not start anything. In order to accomplish any project, the inclination and interest have to be there. Interest is followed by effort, or vigor. If interest is present, it becomes easier to apply ourselves and focus attention on the task at hand. The next factor is intention, by which we mean that the practitioner has made a commitment to develop positive qualities, and work toward overcoming the negative tendencies of the mind. The last factor is analysis, meaning that we have to analyze and see what is beneficial and what is not beneficial for us and others. This is not done by using thinking and concepts in our normal way, which only generates more confusion. Rather, we use our thinking power and conceptual skills to analyze what is beneficial and what is not beneficial.

Buddhism does not discourage thinking, but it does discourage excessive thinking, which doesn't lead us anywhere. Much of the thinking that occupies our mind for twenty-four hours a day is motivated by delusions of excessive attachment, anger, resentment, confusion, pride, ignorance, and so on. We can use our thoughts more constructively than this, which is what we are recommending here.

In this way, the traveler on the spiritual path is able to go through the three stages of the first path, the path of preparation.

The path of preparation establishes us in spiritual practice by turning us away from our everyday concerns to a large extent. Turning away from samsaric preoccupations doesn't necessarily mean that we have to abandon them completely. It is more that we work with the attitude we have toward things and toward other people.

What binds us to the samsaric condition is not things in themselves but our attachment to them, the unceasing craving and grasping that arise in the mind. It is these that we have to work with. Material wealth can become a hindrance, for example, if attachment, clinging, and grasping are present in the mind of the individual.

The sharp distinction between the spiritual and the material that is common in the West is quite foreign to the Buddhist way of thinking. Whether we are spiritual or not is fundamentally dependent on our attitude, how we see the world and how we interact with other sentient beings. The samsaric condition is created not by the external world or conditions that exist outside of ourselves, but by the disturbed mind.

So that's what the path of preparation is all about. We try to train ourselves in such a way that we are able to make progress on the path. It's also called the path of accumulation (of merit), because we can reorient ourselves to become the proper vessel in order to develop further. The idea of being a vessel is very important in Buddhism. It means that if we have been unable to create the appropriate mental conditions to give rise to certain spiritual qualities, then no matter what sort of master or spiritual teacher we are in contact with, no matter which texts we have read and understood, nothing much will happen. This is because we have been unable to create in ourselves a real spiritual vessel that is able to contain the qualities necessary for our development. We need to be open and have a sense of receptivity in our mind-stream. By developing in this way, we are able to embark on the next path, the path of application.

Returning Home

The Bodhisattva perspective on these first two paths differs slightly from the Shravaka one. In addition to the practices shared with the Shravakas, the Bodhisattva is able to generate bodhichitta, or the compassionate concern for all living creatures. This commitment to caring for others actually comes from the way in which the Bodhisattva understands himself or herself, as having Buddha-nature within. From the Bodhisattva perspective, the journey is not necessarily a linear one, in which we leave samsara and arrive at nirvana, but is more like returning home.

If we see our own ego as being the principal source of our identity, this causes feelings of alienation, rejection, and disengagement. But if we begin to realize that our own nature is that of the Buddha, and that everyone else has this same nature, we feel more affinity with other sentient beings.

There are stories in the Mahayana sutras about this process of leaving home and returning home. We got lost by becoming completely enmeshed in the samsaric condition and seeing the ego as our principal source of identity. As we come to realize our own Buddha-nature through practice, we start to find our way home and in fact discover that our home has always been here, but for some reason we have not been able to see it. Instead, we have been taking refuge in an alternative "home" that is not truly our own.

THE PATH OF APPLICATION

The path of application, or path of junction, consists of meditation on the Four Noble Truths—the truth of suffering, the truth of the origin of suffering, the truth of the cessation of suffering, and the path that leads us out of suffering. It is important to understand suffering in order to overcome it. If we do not fully acknowledge that suffering is a reality, it is very unlikely that we will make any real effort to overcome it. So first we must acknowledge the existence of suffering fully and in a realistic manner.

As part of the practice of the path of application there are four meditations, each associated with one of the Four Noble Truths. The four meditations are on suffering, impermanence, emptiness, and selflessness.

The Truth of Suffering

Several meditations are practiced in connection with the first Noble Truth. The first practice is the *meditation on suffering* itself. Three different types of suffering are described in the teachings. One is "conditioned suffering": the fact that everything is subject to change and is the product of causes and conditions naturally produces suffering in us. Particularly when things are pleasant and joyous, we do not want these situations to change. But because everything is subject to change, sooner or later we have to accept the fact that what used to give us pleasure no longer does so, or even becomes the cause of unhappiness. Old age is an example of conditioned suffering. Whether we go to the gym or not, whether we have liposuction or breast implants or go to the plastic surgeon to remove wrinkles, the fact of the matter is that we are getting older. This is something that we have to accept. I'm not saying that people should not try to look more youthful, but they need to be more realistic about such things.

The second kind of suffering is the "suffering of change." This includes our anticipation that if we change our job or change our partner, we will be happy. But because the mind has not changed, the suffering continues.

The third kind is the "suffering of suffering." We are already suffering in some way, then something else goes wrong and we suffer even more. All these types of suffering can be handled if we have done some spiritual practice, because then we are not so overwhelmed by these experiences. But if we have not been trained, we experience real mental anguish and frustration. So we should not think of the Buddhist teachings on suffering as pessimistic or exaggerated. There is no exaggeration, because we all experience this on a daily basis.

The next meditation on the first Noble Truth, the truth of suffering, is the *meditation on impermanence*. When we are suffering, we do not look at the causes and conditions that have given rise to the experience of suffering. We are so engrossed in the experience that we forget that the experience itself is part of the causes and conditions. The intensity of the experience of suffering prevents this insight from occurring.

The third practice is the *meditation on emptiness*. The practitioner has to realize that the experience of suffering itself has no real enduring essence or reality. This comes from the meditation practice I just mentioned, through realizing that suffering is produced by causes and conditions.

The last meditation associated with the truth of suffering is the *meditation on selflessness*. The practitioner has to realize that there is no permanent, unchanging self that is enduring all these unpleasant experiences. The belief that there is something called a "self" or a "soul" that is unchanging and permanent is so strong as to be almost instinctive. Even our language accustoms us to saying things like "my feelings," "my memory," "my body," "my passions," "my emotions," "my thoughts," "my concepts," and we regard the self as something that exists over and above all these things. Buddhist teachings say that this is completely fictitious and fabricated by the mind.

From the Buddhist perspective, the self should be seen as dynamic and alive, not static and fixed. If the self were to be completely unchanging, it would not be affected by whatever goes on in the mind. But if it were untouched by our thoughts, feelings, emotions, and concepts, then what use would the self have, even if it existed?

To be able to experience things in an emotional way and use our thoughts in a creative manner is what makes our life interesting. When we think of ourselves as a fixed entity, when we say, "I was hurt so badly," we are unable to let go. But if we think of ourselves as being in a dynamic process continuously, our fixation on the past will be greatly reduced. Then we can really take charge of our lives. We are able to deal with our present experiences and even reconcile the past, as well as having a greater understanding of how to work with our future situation. This constantly dynamic self is an important idea in Buddhism. Without it we cannot make any spiritual progress at all.

The Origin of Suffering

The next of the Four Noble Truths is the truth of the origin of suffering. According to the Buddhist teachings, the fundamental source of suffering lies within, in our grasping and clinging. These produce suffering. The injustices that exist in the world, the poverty and so on, are also reflections of the individual mind. Fundamentally, all the different kinds of suffering which are experienced in the world have their origin in the mind and are created by clinging and grasping.

The first contemplation on the truth of the origin of suffering involves "causes." Instead of thinking that suffering exists and this is just a fact, we have to look at the causes. We have to see where suffering originates, how it is caused and in what manner it arises. The second is the contemplation of "effect," an inquiry into what sorts of effects are produced by what sorts of causes. The Buddha said that anyone who can really understand the relationship between cause and effect understands his teachings properly. Thus causality is seen as central to Buddhist philosophy.

The third contemplation is the contemplation of "appearance," which means looking at the experience of suffering itself. The last contemplation is on "conditions." There are not only causes present, but conditions also, in order for the effects to come into being.

These four contemplations have one aim in common, which is to correct our understanding of how things happen. For example, many people believe that the first cause, or the final cause, is some form of God. According to the Buddhist teachings, becoming familiar with the contemplations mentioned above corrects the kind of understanding that says that there are first causes or final causes, there is a creator, and so on.

The Cessation of Suffering

The next truth is the truth of cessation. Cessation means that it is possible to end our experience of suffering and mental torment. It is a possibility and it can be done. The first contemplation of this truth involves the "conviction" that impurities of the mind can be eradicated and abandoned. The second consists of the "contemplation of quiescence," which means that suffering can be completely eradicated and that there will be no suffering left when we attain nirvana. We gain complete conviction of the possibility of attaining permanent quiescence.

The third contemplation is that of "excellence," meaning that we realize that shamatha meditation experiences fall short of real spiritual practice. Such meditation is unable to provide the practitioner with the final liberation, which has to come from vipashyana. The fourth contemplation is on "renunciation." This consists of realizing that all the defiling tendencies of the mind can be renounced and that liberation can be attained as a consequence.

The Path Out of Suffering

We now arrive at the three contemplations of the truth of the path. The first involves contemplating the path and seeing it as the vehicle that is capable of transporting us from samsara to nirvana. Not only is it possible to bring suffering to an end, but we realize that there are methods that can be employed in order to do so. And this is what the contemplation of the path consists of. The second contemplation is on attainment, by which we realize that the path we are following is the correct path, and we have no interest in deviating from that. The third contemplation is on liberation. We realize that by following the Eightfold Noble Path we can achieve liberation, and we can go beyond the samsaric condition with which we have become very familiar.

By contemplating the Four Noble Truths in this way, practitioners on the path of application are able to develop through the next four stages.

Four Levels of Attainment

The fundamental insight developed from the practice of the contemplations on the Four Noble Truths is to realize that everything arises from causes and conditions. This insight brings about the first level of the path of application, which is called heat, or *tummo* in Tibetan. *Tummo* in this context is used as a metaphor. Just as heat is an indication of the presence of fire, so when the practitioner has arrived at the first level of the path of application, which is heat, he or she begins to experience the heat of the fire of wisdom or insight.

Just as fire has the capacity to burn wood or debris and to consume it, similarly wisdom has the capacity to consume the defilements and obscurations of the mind. The experience of heat is followed by the second level of the path of application, *tsemo*, which means "summit" or "peak." The practitioner at this level has been able to work with and perfect all the positive qualities of a worldly person.

Until we have been able to attain the third path, which is the path of seeing, whatever we have developed up to that point is still very much involved with what are called the worldly virtues and qualities, rather than the transworldly ones. The reason why the good qualities developed on the level of peak still remain within the realm of mundanity and not supramundanity is that real insight is developed at the level of the path of seeing and not before.

The experience of peak is followed by what is called patience, or *söpa* in Tibetan. This is not patience in the ordinary sense, but is concerned more with fearlessness. The practitioner is no longer afraid of concepts such as impermanence, nonsubstantiality, and emptiness. Instead of thinking of them as something negative or frightening, the practitioner has full confidence in their reality. Real conviction is established, based on an attitude of being completely fearless.

The path of application culminates in the attainment of excellence of the worldly spiritual qualities. This is called *chöchok* in Tibetan, which means "most excellent of dharmas," but in this context it means "dharmas associated with worldly attainments." The experience of supreme or excellent spiritual qualities of the worldly person produces an insight that is very similar to that of someone on the path of seeing.

According to the teachings, once the second level of the path of application has been attained, it is practically impossible for practitioners to regress. Whatever qualities they have been able to develop will remain, and they cannot slip backwards. After the level of patience, it is not possible to fall into lower forms of existence. For example, if you want to become a musician and you practice every day, you become very good at it. After that, even if you do not practice for many years it is easy to pick it up again. But if you have been half-hearted in your practice, and then you neglect it for a few years, when you try to go back to it, you have to virtually start all over again. It's as if you had never learned any music whatsoever. It's the same with Dharma practice. Doing some spiritual practice as often as we can, on a daily basis, is more fruitful than doing a lot of practice for a short time, followed by no practice for a long time.

The experience of supreme or excellent qualities of the worldly spiritual person leads to the realization of the path of seeing. It gets its name from the fact that for the first time the practitioner gains true insight into reality. This path of seeing has been attained because the "five spiritual faculties" have been developed to the utmost level on the third level of the path of application. These faculties are heat, effort, mindfulness, concentration, and insight or wisdom. Just as our physical sense organs and faculties enable us to see the world more clearly and to function better, similarly, we can perceive reality in its true form by developing the five spiritual faculties.

THE PATH OF SEEING

The last level of the path of application is the end of the worldly spiritual path. From here on it is called the "supramundane spiritual path." This starts with the path of seeing. In Mahayana Buddhism, the path of seeing coincides with the first stage, or bhumi, of the Bodhisattva. The reason why this is called the path of seeing is that for the first time the practitioner has come face to face with ultimate reality and sees it for the first time. From now on, whatever one does is unsullied activity. One is not bound by karma anymore, because one's actions do not lead to the creation of further karma.

Insight into Ultimate Reality

In the Shravaka teachings, insight into ultimate reality is gained through formal retreats in which the practitioner undergoes the "sixteen moments of realization"—four associated with each of the Four Noble Truths. A "moment" here does not necessarily mean just one moment of time. It could be more akin to what we normally mean by an event.

The four realizations associated with the first of the Four Noble Truths begin with "patient acceptance" of the reality of suffering, followed by the "dharma knowledge" of the reality of suffering. These are the first two moments, and both are involved with the mind state of what is called the "desire realm."

Then follow the second two moments, which are the subsequent patient acceptance of the nature of suffering, and the subsequent dharma knowledge of the reality of suffering, associated with the realms of form and formlessness. These moments of realization are applied to the other three Noble Truths as well, until sixteen such moments are attained.

The "form" and "formless" realms referred to here mean that the practitioner has been able to attain altered states of consciousness. While the first two moments correspond to the normal state of consciousness (the desire realm), the last two moments correspond to these altered states of consciousness (the form and formless realms).

"Patient acceptance" can be understood as more like "conceptual understanding," and "dharma knowledge" means direct experience, or a "nonconceptual direct knowledge" of the Four Noble Truths. Patient acceptance enables us to remain on the path in an uninterrupted manner, without being sidetracked, and direct experience of reality helps us to come closer to attaining liberation.

Even though all this may seem a bit complicated, I think it is important to cover it in the way in which it is discussed in the teachings. This is how the Shravaka practitioner realizes ultimate reality on the path of seeing.

The Bodhisattva path of seeing occurs when the Bodhisattva attains the first level, or *bhumi*. He or she gains insight into ultimate reality, which is shunyata. As I mentioned previously, "emptiness" or "voidness" in the Mahayana teaching does not refer to things not existing or being empty as we normally understand it. Rather, emptiness means that nothing has any kind of enduring substance or essence. The nature of the phenomenal world itself is emptiness. An intimate relationship exists between ultimate truth, which is emptiness, and relative truth, which is the empirical world. Chandrakirti has said that without relying on relative truth we will not understand ultimate truth. Therefore, we should not say that this empirical world is completely illusory and nonexistent. That is not the Mahayanist view of emptiness. To recapitulate further, to think that everything has substantial or inherent existence is to fall into the other extreme. That's why it is said that in order to understand emptiness one has to develop the middle view, the view that does not fall into either extreme of eternalism or nihilism.

We are normally unable to perceive things in their true perspective. Some kind of distortion has been introduced either in terms of our visual organs or in terms of the mind. The teachings present examples such as mistaking a rope for a snake. The rope is there, but to think that the rope is a snake is to misperceive it. Similarly, to think that things have some kind of inherent existence is to misapprehend or misperceive their reality. At the same time, to think that there is nothing at all is to completely misunderstand what is meant by emptiness.

The difference between realizing nonsubstantiality and realizing emptiness is not a difference of kind but of degree. According to the teachings, the Bodhisattva, who understands emptiness, has a more subtle understanding of the nature of things than the Shravaka, who understands nonsubstantiality. Nonsubstantiality is realized through contemplation of causality. If we become very familiar with how the causal nexus operates, our understanding of the nonsubstantiality of things is greatly increased, and from that comes realization of emptiness. Otherwise, we may still cling to some idea of a creator, for example, or to the notion that change is more like transformation and that there is an unchanging reality or substance.

Various theories of atomism say that gross objects like tables and chairs do change, but they are constructed of atoms and these atoms do not change. So it is believed that atoms in themselves have some kind of substantial existence. However, if we become familiar with Buddhist ideas of causality and emptiness, we can see that such theories of atomism are very misleading. That's why Nagarjuna said that because of emptiness, everything is possible. If things had a fixed essence, change would be impossible. Without change, nothing could happen. So, instead of thinking of emptiness as negative, we should consider that it is because of emptiness that the world can function at all. Emptiness makes it possible.

The Seven Limbs of Enlightenment

The Bodhisattva on the first level realizes emptiness for the first time, by realizing the seven limbs of enlightenment. These consist of mindfulness, awareness, discriminating wisdom, effort, joy, concentration, and equanimity. These qualities in the seven limbs exist before they are realized on the path of seeing, but at this stage they are able to mature. From the Shravaka perspective, these qualities are developed from the practice of shamatha, vipashyana and contemplation of the Four Noble Truths. From the Bodhisattva perspective, they develop from the practice of the six paramitas. Having these qualities helps in terms of understanding ultimate reality, but having a greater understanding of ultimate reality would also help in the development of these qualities.

These qualities have to be developed over a period of time. This is why the whole idea of training or cultivation is so important in the Buddhist teachings. We have to learn. We have to educate ourselves. We have to train. Only then will such qualities be actualized. It's not very helpful to have an "all or nothing" attitude here. We should always think in terms of degree. We are either more mindful or less mindful, more aware or less aware; we exert ourselves to a greater or lesser degree, and so forth. If we think that we should have all these qualities fully developed at the very beginning, we are expecting too much of ourselves. If that were the case, the five paths would be redundant!

In Buddhism, it is knowledge that delivers us from the samsaric state of dissatisfaction, frustration, and mental torment, rather than the development of faith or good works. That does not mean that we should not do good works, of course, but they are not sufficient in themselves to obtain liberation. When both good works and compassion are supported by wisdom, practitioners have been able to fulfill both the necessary and sufficient conditions to attain enlightenment. When practitioners attain the path of seeing, they become completely transformed, which is why the path of seeing is equated with the attainment of the supramundane level of spiritual realization.

Until practitioners have arrived at the level of the path of seeing, they have been more involved with creating knowledge, with doing good works, and also perhaps with a certain amount of meditation. They have not been able to develop any insight into the true nature of things until they reach the level of the path of seeing, where they have direct experience of how things really are, rather than how they appear to the deluded consciousness through the senses.

THE PATH OF MEDITATION

The path of seeing is followed by the path of meditation. This coincides with the second stage of the Bodhisattva and stretches to the tenth Bodhisattva level. Although one engages in the practice of meditation right from the beginning, starting from the path of preparation, on the path of meditation one starts to gain certain experiences and realizations that were not present previously.

The Dhyanas and Formless Attainments of Shamatha

Through the practice of shamatha, we are able to gain access to areas of consciousness that were previously inaccessible, such as the four levels of *dhyanas*, or meditative concentrations, and the four levels of absorption. The four dhyanas are progressive stages of concentration. At first, thoughts, concepts, and other elements are present as well as emotional experiences of joy and happiness. As we proceed, the mind becomes very settled and concentrated, to such a point that even these mental processes cease to operate. The four stages of concentration correspond to our normal state of consciousness. The four absorptions correspond to the higher reaches of our development in terms of meditation; nevertheless, by themselves they are not necessarily very spiritual. They are simply altered states of consciousness of which we were unaware before.

Through meditation we can experience sensations of happiness and bliss, but on the fourth dhyana level even these cease. They are followed by the first absorption, which is called infinite space, or *namkha thaye* in Tibetan. *Namkha thaye* means that we are in such a deep state of concentration that our senses are no longer operating. We do not see, hear or taste anything, and that is why this state is known as infinite space. This does not mean that things have ceased to exist. It simply means that we have been able to place our mind in such a deep state of concentration that all the gross levels of mental functioning and sensory impressions have been temporarily suspended.

The experience of infinite space is followed by the experience of infinite consciousness, which is *namshe thaye* in Tibetan. Infinite consciousness here means that as we go deeper into the state of consciousness, we see that everything is actually consciousness; there is no sense of duality between subject and object.

The third level of absorption is called *chiyang mepa* in Tibetan, which means "nonexistence." The state of absorption has become deeper so that we really have absolutely no experience, no feelings, no emotions, no thoughts or concepts arising in the mind; so there is nothing.

The last state of absorption is known as "nonperception," which is even deeper than the one before when we were already feeling that there was nothing; it is as though that is not good enough! We have to have another state, when we don't even have the perception of nonperception. "Nonperception" is *yömin memin* ("neither existence nor nonexistence") in Tibetan, which means that, unlike the previous state, we are not even thinking that there is nothing. Even that thought has been dropped.

The Four Divine Abodes and Vipashyana

As I said before, the practice of shamatha may be able to give rise to different levels of consciousness, in which our concentration becomes more focused, but by itself it is unable to create any real spiritual qualities within the mind-stream of the individual. These have to come from the contemplation of the four divine abodes of love, compassion, joy, and equanimity, as well as from vipashyana practice on emptiness, nonsubstantiality, and so forth. Shamatha produces stability of the mind. Based on that stability, we can work with our emotions through the four divine abodes and work with our thoughts and concepts through the practice of vipashyana. Then we are able to transform our meditation so that what we achieve through the practice of meditation becomes supramundane.

In Buddhism it is considered okay to go into altered states of consciousness, but even if we are unable to attain these states we can still attain enlightenment. Certain people have the capacity to go into altered states, but such states are not necessary on the path. What is necessary is that through the practice of shamatha we learn to stabilize our mind. Without mental stability the mind is constantly busy and distracted, either through the senses or in terms of mental activities, emotions, and thoughts. A certain level of mental stability helps to bring about insight, which is essential. Insight meditation causes spiritual transformation in the practitioner, and shamatha meditation, in which mental stability is developed, provides the general conditions that allow insight to arise. That is why both types of meditation are necessary.

When discussing the four divine abodes, we should be clear about our understanding of the words used. Feeling is *tsorwa* in Tibetan and *vedana* in Sanskrit, and has to be distinguished from emotions. Whereas emotions can be skillful or unskillful, feelings cannot. Feelings are closely associated with the body, while emotions are partly physical and partly mental. In the West this idea is very new. In philosophy and in theology, emotions have been closely associated with the body and are therefore thought to be something that we have to learn to control, rather than being related to the mind.

Buddhism says that it is possible to work with emotions in a positive way, because there is nothing intrinsically wrong with them. The problem lies in how we deal with them, how we experience and express them. So we can train ourselves and develop skills in order to use emotions to enliven us and make our lives richer, instead of causing more problems for ourselves and other people. We can learn to create a more positive environment, and this is what contemplation on the four divine abodes involves.

The Bodhisattva experience of the path of meditation relates to the rest of the ten levels, or bhumis, of the Bodhisattva path. Through this path, the Bodhisattva is able to perfect each of the six paramitas—generosity, moral precepts, patience, vigor, concentration and wisdom—as he or she traverses the different levels of bodhisattva attainment. The early perfections are realized first, because it is easier to practice generosity that it is to practice patience, for example. Through training, the Bodhisattva gradually realizes the real extent and potential of the virtues associated with the six perfections. He or she then attains Buddhahood, since the realization of the six paramitas is equated with Buddhahood. Once the tenth Bodhisattva level is attained, the practitioner has become a fully enlightened being or Buddha. He or she has then attained the Bodhisattva ideal of the path of no more learning.

Having traversed the paths and stages described previously, the practitioner attains the last of the five paths, the path of no more learning, which equates with the full enlightenment of Buddhahood. The practitioner has realized the aspects of Buddha's being, referred to as the three *kayas*, which are two aspects of Buddha's being associated with his form body and one aspect associated with his authentic original being. Through the accumulation of merit one realizes the form aspects of Buddha's being and accumulation of wisdom, while on the path one realizes the formless aspect, which is the original state of Buddha's being.

The five paths are part of the teachings called *lamrim*, the path and stages, or *sa lam*, meaning the path and bhumis, or spiritual levels. What is presented here is the idea of spiritual progress. We begin our journey as ordinary, confused sentient beings, our minds completely governed by ignorance and defilements. Gradually purification of the mind takes place, as wisdom and insight increase and our defilements and delusions begin to subside and dissipate. Eventually there is no longer any confusion in the mind; wisdom has flowered and matured in the form of Buddha's mind.

The teachings of the path and stages are presented in a very progressive and developmental form. This approach in called *rimgyipa* in Tibetan, which means a step-by-step approach. But this is not the only approach to the path. There is another one, *chikcharwa* in Tibetan, in which the possibility of sudden illumination is emphasized. The Kagyü tradition, the tradition to which we belong, makes use of both approaches. For example, Gampopa employs the method of the gradualists in his work *The Jewel Ornament of Liberation*, which is a very important text for our Kagyü tradition. At the same time there is another strand of the tradition, coming from the Mahamudra teachings, which emphasizes the sudden illumination approach. So it is necessary for us to be able to reconcile the differences between these two approaches.

We need to understand that the path and stages as presented in the Sutra teachings should not be taken too literally. For example, it is said in the sutras that a Bodhisattva must remain in the samsaric world for three countless eons before Buddhahood is attained. Even Buddha-nature—the potential for enlightenment that exists in the mind-stream of the individual—is sometimes regarded as a potentiality rather than an actuality in the Sutra tradition. According to this perspective, to actualize it means that we must engage in the path of the Bodhisattva and traverse all the different stages of this path in order to accomplish Buddhahood. Thus the concept of Buddha-nature is seen as a potentiality that has to be brought to the surface through a long period of practice. It can't be attained instantaneously, according to the Sutra teachings. However, as we shall see when we turn to a discussion of the Tantra and Mahamudra traditions, this is not the view of all the Buddhist schools.

12

BUDDHAHOOD

The Three Kayas

TWO TYPES OF BUDDHA'S BEING

The idea of the three *kayas* is associated with the ultimate aspiration of practitioners. It symbolizes the final goal that they would like to achieve. Generally, we talk about the two levels of truth, the ground as the starting point, the two accumulations of wisdom and means as the path, and the two types of Buddha's being (kaya) as the fruition. As a starting point, we begin to look at our perception of the world and our perception of ourselves. We realize that so many of our experiences are conceptual constructions. There is no reality to them because they are insubstantial. With that realization, we have some insight into absolute truth. In this sense, one uses the idea of two levels of truth as the starting point. When we embark upon the path, the idea of working for the benefit of others becomes important. This is achieved through engaging in Bodhisattva deeds such as generating compassion. This sows the seeds for attaining the "form body" of the Buddha (*rupakaya*). Concurrently, as one also increases one's insight and wisdom, this eventually manifests as the full unfoldment of the "formless aspect" of Buddha's being (*arupakaya*). The formless aspect is called *dharmakaya*. The three kayas are an expansion of two kayas, because both the *sambhogakaya* and *nirmanakaya* are subsumed under the "form body," while the dharmakaya is the "formless" aspect. Therefore, we essentially have two aspects of Buddha's being, or two aspects of enlightenment. It is the realization of these aspects that are the basic goal or the basic aim of the practitioner.

ONE EXISTENTIAL STATE

Now, the idea of three bodies should not mislead us into thinking that there is some kind of entity, or three different kinds of entities, that are being spoken of here. Dharmakaya (the formless body) and sambhogakaya (one of the form bodies) do not refer to any kind of entity as such, but more to a certain existential state of being. As far as the idea of dharmakaya or formless body is concerned, this is something that is always present. Dharmakaya is only rediscovered. It is not something that is created or made to manifest anew. And the same can be said of the sambhogakaya aspect, which has more to do with the mind's ability to manifest in a way that is able to express all potentialities in relation to the five wisdoms. As such, the sambhogakaya aspect is related to the mental powers.

The nirmanakaya aspect is the only one that has been created anew. The nirmanakaya is the result of having purified one's body, speech, and mind. In this way, one's physical body ceases to be a locus of all kinds of undesirable negative tendencies, such as excessive desire. Instead, it becomes a medium that can have extraordinary power for working with others and benefiting others. Therefore, nirmanakaya is the physical aspect of an enlightened being. It is said to be new because it is something different.

As far as the sambhogakaya and dharmakaya aspects are concerned, they are already embodied within each sentient being. It is a matter of whether one is able to come to a realization of them or not.

TWOFOLD PURITY OF THE DHARMAKAYA

Dharmakaya is the embodiment of what is called twofold purity. One aspect of the dharmakaya is completely empty, completely open. It has never been corrupted by experiences of emotional conflict and conceptual confusion. So there is a primordial sense of purity. As we begin to become cleansed of the defilements on the path, through working with our emotional conflicts and conceptual confusions, we develop the temporary aspect of the purity of the dharmakaya.

When we start to realize the twofold purity, we can also manifest in sambhogakaya form. However, sambhogakaya is not something that can be perceived by ordinary beings. We would need to have a purified mind to perceive the sambhogakaya aspect and to communicate that. Although a person may be manifesting all kinds of mental powers, if the audience is limited in its capacity and subject to all kinds of illusions, it will not be able to appreciate the sambhogakaya manifestation. That is why the Buddhas always work through the nirmanakaya aspect, because the nirmanakaya enables a Buddha to operate physically for the benefit of others. A Buddha is able to communicate verbally and mentally through his or her physical expressions, which is the nirmanakaya aspect.

We should not think that these three kayas are completely independent of one another. They are interrelated, and when they have become fully unfolded, they are inseparable. The form aspects of the sambhogakaya and nirmanakaya manifest out of dharmakaya. Both form bodies are therefore dependent on the formless body, because that is the origin upon which these other two form bodies are grounded. The dharmakaya refers to an undifferentiated state of being. We cannot talk about either the state of confusion or the state of enlightenment in reference to it, because the dharmakaya is in a sense atemporal and ahistorical. Nor can we attribute change or transformation to it, because dharmakaya is a state of being that is totally indeterminate.

Because of its indeterminateness, the dharmakaya can give rise to certain deterministic characteristics or aspects. Thus, we have the sambhogakaya and nirmanakaya arising out of the dharmakaya. Because the dharmakaya is passive in nature, it cannot manifest as a good medium for working with others and for their benefit. This is accomplished through the realization of the sambhogakaya and nirmanakaya. The reason why these are called "form bodies" is not that they are actual physical bodies, but that they manifest and are determinate, in contrast to dharmakaya, which is immaterial and indeterminate.

The sambhogakaya is determinate because it manifests in a variety of ways. This does not mean that the sambhogakaya is not physical, however. The sambhogakaya does give rise to nirmanakaya, and this last kaya is physical in its essence. The nirmanakaya is therefore the manifestation of being, the embodiment of the other two kayas. The sambhogakaya realization can manifest through nirmanakaya, because the nirmanakaya is historically situated. We can talk about Buddha Shakyamuni attaining enlightenment in Bodhgaya, proceeding to give teachings in Varanasi, and eventually attaining *parinirvana* (complete enlightenment at death) in Kushinagar, because we are describing the Buddha Shakyamuni in his nirmanakaya aspect. However, we cannot attribute any kind of temporality to the sambhogakaya and dharmakaya aspects because they are not historically situated. They are always manifesting and ever-present.

The primordial sense of the sambhogakaya aspect is symbolized by the Vajradhara, the Primordial Buddha who is a representation of ultimate reality. He is the holder of the scepter, or *vajra*, which signifies the perennial truthfulness of reality. It is not subjected to change and transformation, and does not need to be updated. The vajra cannot be made into something that is relative or conditional because it is perennially true. Therefore, "holder" delineates the importance of possessing this, of being able to hold the perennial truthfulness of reality.

SAMBHOGAKAYA

Sambhogakaya is called *longchö dzokpe ku* in Tibetan. *Longchö* means "to make use of" or "to indulge," *dzokpe* means "perfect bliss," and *ku* means "body." Therefore, the sambhogakaya realm is the state of blissfulness. It is always immersed in a state of unceasing bliss. It is said that the sambhogakaya does not manifest in any kind of spatial or physical location. It manifests in a place called Akanistha (Ogmin), which is not really a place, because it is not located anywhere. *Ogmin* means "not underneath." It is a place that is nowhere, that is all-encompassing. As such, Ogmin or Akanistha refers to emptiness (shunyata). The teacher Vajradhara manifests in Akanishtha. However, the sambhogakaya does not embody the ordinary teachings of the three yanas, but the most essential teachings of the supreme Tantrayana. These teachings are perennially meaningful, because the significance of the teachings is not relative to historical situations.

This sambhogakaya aspect is only perceptible to advanced people who are endowed with extraordinarily lucid and perceptive minds. Thus, the audiences of this Akanistha realm are only those beings of advanced realization. From the point of view of the nirmanakaya aspect however, there is a historical personage who presented the teachings of the three yanas in a particular physical location. In this context then, the audience would also be constituted of beings with various capacities, dispositions and inclinations.

However, it is said that we can only make this distinction between sambhogakaya and nirmanakaya from an outside perspective. In terms of the experience of the Buddha himself, we cannot talk about one preceding the other, or of the sambhogakaya being superior to the nirmanakaya. Nor can we say that the sambhogakaya manifested first and the Buddha only realizes the nirmanakaya aspect afterward. However, if we look at it conceptually, we can make a distinction between the two, although this distinction is impossible to make at the experiential level of reality.

The sambhogakaya aspect is also endowed with the so-called five auspicious coincidences (*phünsum tspa*). The first auspicious coincidence is that of *place*, meaning that the sambhogakaya manifests in the place of Akanishtha. The second auspicious coincidence is the emergence of the Buddha, or physical *teacher*. In this particular case, it is the nirmanakaya aspect being spoken of, or the physical teacher who is endowed with all kinds of qualities. The third auspicious coincidence is the manifestation of the *teachings*. In this case the teachings refer to the pure essence of tantric manifestations, which are not even presented in written scriptural form. If the meaning of these essential instructions are practiced and realized, the state of enlightenment can be attained in one lifetime. The fourth auspicious coincidence is the convergence of the proper *audience*. This audience consists of such beings as Bodhisattvas, *dakas* and *dakinis* (spiritually advanced male and female beings), and others that are advanced on the path. The fifth auspicious coincidence is *time*. This is a complicated condition because in terms of the sambhogakaya teachings, unlike the nirmanakaya, the past, present, and future are not a relevant conceptual framework. We cannot talk about them in terms of history. We can say that the teachings of the Buddha's nirmanakaya aspect were given at a certain historical point, and we can even speculate that these teachings might cease to exist at some point. However, we cannot say that in reference to the teachings that the sambhogakaya embodies, because these are not related to any historical phenomenon. The sambhogakaya teachings are ever present and therefore unceasing.

The sambhogakaya has certain qualities in relation to the auspicious coincidence of the teacher. One of these is called the "qualities of the limbs." Unlike the nirmanakaya aspect, one cannot talk about the sambhogakaya ceasing to exist. The following seven limbs are therefore what distinguish the qualities of the sambhogakaya from that of the nirmanakaya, which is the other form body of the Buddha.

1. The limb of immersion: The sambhogakaya aspect is fully immersed in the Mahayana teachings.
2. The limb of coexistence: The sambhogakaya aspect has never been corrupted, and therefore manifests in conjunction with wisdom.
3. The limb of fullness: The sambhogakaya aspect is completely immersed in the truth.
4. The limb of nonsubstantiality: The sambhogakaya is not substantial and is lacking in inherent existence.
5. The limb of infinite compassion: The sambhogakaya aspect is fully imbued with compassionate concerns, which manifest from the dharmakaya aspect. Through being imbued in compassion, it directs its attention toward other sentient beings.
6. The limb of noncessation: The sambhogakaya's resonating concern for other sentient beings is ever-present and unceasing.
7. The limb of perennial manifestation: The sambhogakaya cannot cease to be and manifests throughout the ages.

Traditionally it is said that the relationship between dharmakaya, sambhogakaya, and nirmanakaya is like the sky, the clouds and the rain. The sky corresponding to the dharmakaya aspect, the clouds to the sambhogakaya aspect, and the rain to the nirmanakaya manifestation. In the same way that space or the sky is not a conditioned product, the dharmakaya is also an unconditioned thing. It has not come about because of causes and conditions, and is therefore an indeterminate state. However, just as space gives rise to cloud formations, the dharmakaya gives rise to the various manifestations of the sambhogakaya.

An example of the way that Buddhists have understood the dharmakaya can be found in the text *Dü ma che (Asamskara)*, which says that the dharmakaya is a state that precedes both confusion and wisdom. It exists before any dualistic notions have arisen. This means that even before one experiences anything, there is this state of dharmakaya, this unconditional state which has arisen spontaneously, not as the product of causes and conditions. This state is neutral because it is neither positive nor negative; the idea of duality does not apply here. Yet at the same time there is the presence of self-awareness. This state of dharmakaya has never been corrupted by emotional conflicts or conceptual confusions. Therefore, one cannot talk in terms of either nirvana or samsara in relation to it. Before we had any idea of Buddhas or sentient beings, there was a state that was absolutely pure, uncorrupted, and self-aware. This dharmakaya is the basis or matrix of all experiences that manifest. It does not matter whether one is a being in the hell realms or a Buddha; the presence of this particular substratum or matrix is the same. Dharmakaya is the nondifferentiated state, the basic source for the manifestation of our conscious experiences.

Dharmakaya as a state is not an entity; it is not a thing. It is unconditional, and it is permanent. This is why it is said that dharmakaya is not a product of causes and conditions. Nevertheless, when the dharmakaya is described as permanent, this does not mean that there is an entity that endures forever. The dharmakaya is not an entity; it is nothing and cannot be said to be permanent in this way. It is permanent in the same sense as the sky can be said to be permanent. The sky is permanent because it is unconditional; it has never arisen and therefore cannot cease to exist.

This nonconditional state gives rise to all the conditional experiences of samsara and nirvana, confusion and wisdom, as well as conceptual perplexities, emotional conflicts, and so on. These various manifestations of the mind are related to the sambhogakaya aspect, which also manifests from this nondifferentiated state. Therefore, working with one's mind via the visualization of deities, the utterance of mantras, and so on, is also a way of trying to invoke the sambhogakaya energy. If one is successful with these practices one can have different kinds of visions, even visitations of many kinds. The sambhogakaya can manifest in certain significant or symbolic situations in one's life. The story of Naropa is an excellent example of this experience. Naropa was a professor at Nalanda University in India. The story goes that at one time Naropa was taking a walk when he encountered the ugliest woman he had ever set eyes on. She asked him if he knew the Buddhist teachings. He answered in the affirmative, saying that he was a professor at Nalanda University. She started to sing and dance in response to this answer, which puzzled Naropa. Then she asked him whether he knew the meaning of the Buddhist teachings. However, this time when he said yes, the old woman began to cry and wail. Then it clicked with him that all his understanding was purely intellectual or conceptual and that he had completely neglected his intuitive side. The ugly old woman represented the emotional or intuitive aspects of his mind. This vision was a symbolic calling from the dimension of the sambhogakaya, a revelatory experience of some kind.

One can have a variety of experiences of this nature in terms of the sambhogakaya aspect. It is said that the sambhogakaya communicates in symbolic language and manifests not through words, descriptions, and explanations, but through intuitive responses to experiences. Visions and dreams are an example of that whole symbolic language. In this context there is another list related to the sambhogakaya aspect, in addition to the seven limbs mentioned above. These are the eight types of power and enrichment (*wangchuk gye*).

1. The power and enrichment of the body (*ku yi wangchuk*) means that the power of the body becomes so great that all things of

a samsaric and nirvanic nature become completely subdued. One takes full charge of them and is enriched by all the qualities and positive things that come of this.

2. The power and enrichment of speech (*sung gi wangchuk*) means that the capacity of communication is able to assimilate all the essential verbal elements of both samsara and nirvana. One becomes enriched and empowered by being able to make full use of them.

3. The power and enrichment of the mind (*thuk kyi wangchuk*) means that one is able to integrate the mental powers in relation to both samsara and nirvana. One becomes empowered and enriched with all the different possibilities of mental manifestation.

4. The power and enrichment of miracle (*dzutrül kyi wangchuk*) means that the capacity to use the three gates of body, speech, and mind is such that one is no longer confined by conventional modes of expression. One is able to go beyond them and display power in unusual ways.

5. The empowerment and enrichment that is ever-going (*küntu dro wangchuk*) means that one is constantly being impelled toward action, toward intention in terms of accomplishing things for the benefit of others. Again, one becomes fully endowed with varieties of powers related to samsaric and nirvanic qualities.

6. The empowerment and enrichment of place (*ne kyi wangchuk*) means that the sambhogakaya is situated in Akanistha, the basic sphere of reality. So one becomes enriched and empowered in that sense because sambhogakaya is inseparably united with reality.

7. The empowerment and enrichment of sensuality (*dö-pe wangchuk*) is connected with the idea that sambhogakaya is inseparably in unison with its feminine counterpart. Whether one calls that the Mother of All Buddhas, the selflessness one, Vajravarahi, or Vajrayogini, it is always continuously in unison with the sambhogakaya. The Sambhogakaya experience is continuously producing the great bliss of being in unison, which is the Mahamudra expression as well. One is empowered and enriched by the capacity to manifest wisdom, or prajna (*sherap*).

8. The empowerment and enrichment of the fulfillment of one's wishes (*kye dö-pe wangchuk*) means that the sambhogakaya is intrinsically endowed with all the worldly and supermundane boons.

Worldly boons (*lokasiddha*) refer to capacities such as extrasensory perception, clairvoyance, clairaudience, and telepathy. These abilities are the result different spiritual realizations.

NIRMANAKAYA

If one is able to tune in to the sambhogakaya, one is able to manifest in nirmanakaya form. It is said that there are three different kinds of nirmanakaya. These are the nirmanakaya of artifacts (*zo yi tulku*), the nirmanakaya of birth (*kyewe tulku*), and the nirmanakaya of the absolute (*chok ki tulku*). The nirmanakaya of artifacts refers to statues and other sacred objects venerated as religious symbols. The nirmanakaya of birth refers to the highly evolved beings that continue to reincarnate for the benefit of others. This is why the tulkus (incarnations) are called tulkus, because they manifest in certain nirmanakaya forms to benefit others. The nirmanakaya of the absolute refers to people who have fully realized Buddhahood. So nirmanakaya can manifest in these different ways.

FOUR MODES OF COMPASSION

Both the nirmanakaya and sambhogakaya are directed toward helping others. Once one has been able to give birth to enlightenment, one becomes automatically moved and impelled to work for the benefit of others. People often ask how we can work for the benefit of others when we have completely overcome dualistic notions of all kinds. For then there is no distinction between the object of compassion and the agent who practices compassion. Some people have seen a problem here because such actions suggest that the Buddha must still be subject to dualistic notions, thinking that there are sentient beings that exist as objects for his compassion. Traditionally however, it is said that there is no real problem here because a Buddha's awareness of sentient beings as an object of compassion is not the result of dualistic thought. The Buddha does not generate compassion based upon deliberation and planning. In what manner, then, is a Buddha's compassion generated? It is said there are four modes in which the nirmanakaya and sambhogakaya manifest compassion.

The first is called the ever-present manifestation of compassion. This means that compassion is part of the property of realization of sambhogakaya. Compassion has always been there; it can never be exhausted or said only to manifest at a particular point. In that sense, the compassion of the sambhogakaya is inexhaustible. Even if the Buddha passes into parinirvana, the manifestation of compassion does not cease. Because even if the nirmanakaya stops manifesting for a while, the awakened energy continues to manifest at the sambhogakaya level. For instance, it is said in the sutras that from the sambhogakaya point of view, the Buddhas do not pass into parinirvana. Dharmas do not cease to be propounded, because on the level of sambhogakaya the teachings remain embodied in the sambhogakaya experience. The nirmanakaya form only manifests and dissolves in order to benefit sentient beings that are subject to laziness. There is no such coming into being or going out of existence on the sambhogakaya level however. So the manifestation of compassion is ever-present.

The second mode is called compassion that manifests spontaneously without any provocation. This manifestation of compassion is described as resonating concern. It is said that compassion arises in response to certain situations without any judgment, without any conceptual interpretation, and without being based upon concerns of that nature. The image is given of the sun illuminating the darkness, or the moon being reflected in water. Compassion is ever-present in this way. It manifests spontaneously and automatically without compulsion or without being elicited.

The third mode is called compassion in terms of meeting the appropriate object. Only beings able to respond to the sambhogakaya manifestation receive this compassion. Therefore, the object of compassion and the kind of compassion they receive correspond with one another. The compassion of the sambhogakaya and the compassion of the nirmanakaya manifest in a way that is appropriate for the types of people who are there. In this way the different beings, with their different dispositions and predilections, are able to receive that compassion depending on their level of understanding and evolvement.

The fourth mode is compassion that has been requested. This

type of compassion has two aspects, the compassionate response that has been elicited in a general way and the compassion that has been elicited in a more specific way. Eliciting a compassionate response in a general way means that the enlightened being who is manifesting as the sambhogakaya aspect in emptiness is stirred from this state because of compassion. In other words, compassion keeps the Buddha active in the world. The compassionate response that has been elicited in a more specific way is compassion that arises in response to actual situations in this particular world. For instance, when the Buddha attained enlightenment, he did not automatically start to teach. He had to be requested to teach and to work for the benefit of others. In that way his compassion manifested. It is said that any requests for compassion from the lama or the yidam is compassion manifesting in a specific way.

Two Aspects of Buddha's Teaching

We see, therefore, that compassion can manifest in relation to both the sambhogakaya and the nirmanakaya in those four modes. The by-product of the sambhogakaya manifestation of compassion is the compassion that manifests in the public arena through the medium of the nirmanakaya. This is related to the teachings that an enlightened being gives, because the ultimate form of compassion is said to be the teachings. Teachings from a Buddhist point of view have two aspects. One is called *ka,* which are the teachings that the Buddha gave from his own mouth. The other one is called *tenjur,* which are the commentarial exegeses based upon the Buddha's own teachings.

The *ka* has three aspects. The first aspect is the teachings that the Buddha literally gave (*shal ne sungpe ka*) and the second is the teachings inspired by the Buddha in his presence (*chin gyi lape ka*). The latter category means that even though the Buddha was present at the time, he did not literally give the teachings himself, but encouraged or inspired someone who was also present—such as Avalokiteshvara—to act as a mouthpiece for himself. Therefore, although Buddha did not literally give the teachings, they have the same authority as the Buddha's own teachings, just as if they had been given by his own mouth. Finally, we have the teachings that were bequeathed to another generation of practitioners (*jesu nangwe ka*). These teachings were not really presented during the Buddha's own lifetime but were invoked, rediscovered, or given a new impetus by another generation. However, it is as if the basic impetus came from the Buddha himself.

The *tenjur*, or commentarial exegeses, have two aspects. One is the doctrinal aspect and the other is the experiential aspect. These two aspects must correspond. If one has studied the teachings and learned them intellectually, those teachings must then be made to correspond with one's inner experiences. There is no single doctrine that we could call the definitive teaching of Buddhism. It is said that through his infinite wisdom, compassion, and exercise of skillful means, the Buddha was able to devise many kinds of methods and many interpretations. However, there are many levels of interpretation, and many levels of understanding. As Nagarjuna says, "The dharma of the Buddha is immense, like the ocean. Depending on the aptitudes of beings, it is expounded in various ways. Sometimes it speaks of existence, and sometimes it speaks of non-existence. Sometimes it speaks of eternity, other times of impermanence. Sometimes happiness, other times suffering. Sometimes the self, other times the not-self," and so on. Then he goes on to say, "Such are the manifold and diverse teachings of the Buddha."

THREE TURNINGS OF THE WHEEL OF DHARMA

In the early Hinayana teachings—referred to as the first turning of the Wheel of Dharma—the Buddha negated the existence of a permanent substantial self, but did not go into an elaborate discussion of this in relation to emptiness. In the second turning of the Wheel of Dharma, the teachings of the emptiness of phenomena are introduced. Here there is both the idea of the nonsubstantiality or emptiness of the self, as well as emptiness of external phenomena. Then in the third turning of the Wheel of Dharma, the idea of tathagatagarbha, or Buddha-nature, is introduced. In these teachings the negation of an inherently existing self or ego or soul, is integrated with an incorruptible spiritual principle called the tathagatagarbha, the Buddha-nature that remains untainted by the passions and conceptual confusions of the mind.

So different levels of teachings are given. Sometimes these teachings may seem to contradict one another and even counter each other's propositions. However, it is said that the teachings are presented that way in order to reach the widest audience. People require teachings appropriate to their different levels of understanding, aptitudes, and dispositions. Buddha gave teachings in such a way that the meaning could be understood on many different levels. The Mahayana way of solving the problem of which teachings contain the essential meaning of Buddhism, and which are really peripheral and superficial, was to introduce the distinction between interpretive teachings and definitive teachings.

The interpretive teachings are called *trangdön* (*niyartha*). *Trang* means "liberate"; *dön* means "meaning." These teachings contain meanings that have been given with the intention of liberating others. These should not necessarily be taken literally, but they do have their own functions. For example, all kinds of far-fetched, extraordinary, and incredible stories are told in the sutras and shastras about the miraculous activities of bodhisattvas. There are teachings in which the Buddha may have even said that there is a self, or something of that nature. These are said to be interpretive teachings because they are told in order to inspire people. Their meaning therefore needs to be understood in this context.

The definitive teachings are called *ngedön* (*nitartha*). These teachings are generally concerned with emptiness. All the teachings that discourse on emptiness should be taken literally. From the Mahayana point of view, all the teachings that are concerned with emptiness should be taken as definitive, and all the others should be taken as interpretive.

However, there is still a problem here because not all the different schools of Buddhism agree upon which teachings are interpretive and which teachings are definitive. There is some kind of disagreement in Tibetan Buddhism, for example. The Kagyü and Nyingma traditions of Tibetan Buddhism understand the teachings on tathagata-garbha—which were presented in the third turning of the Wheel of Dharma—as the ultimate meaning. However, the Gelugpas would say that these teachings on Buddha-nature are not definite in meaning. For them, the tathagatagarbha teachings were only given so that people would not freak out at the thought that they do not have a substantial ego. Therefore, the tathagatagarbha only has an interpretive meaning in their system.

Anyway, all of these different varieties of teachings—as complex as they may be—are given only in order to alleviate people's suffering and neurosis. It is said that there are 84,000 different types of teachings, which correspond to 84,000 different kinds of neuroses. However, all the teachings are supposed to alleviate people's sufferings. They are all oriented toward realization of the three kayas, or three modes of Buddha's being.

13

SUTRA AND TANTRA

The Tantric Levels of Attainment

IT IS IMPORTANT TO UNDERSTAND the Sutra tradition of Mahayana, because it is impossible to understand Tantra without first having grasped the sutric concepts. While there is no difference in terms of the objective of followers of Sutra and Tantra, the tantric teachings are said to be superior to the sutric teachings in certain important respects.

The Sutra approach to Mahayana is gradual and gentle, using certain methods over a period of time to approach the goal. Tantra, however, is confrontational, more disturbing, and with quicker results precisely because of that. For these reasons, the sutric Mahayana is called the "causal yana," or the vehicle of the cause, and the tantric form of Mahayana is called the "resultant yana."

The followers of both Sutra and Tantra aim to achieve the state called "nonabiding nirvana." This term indicates the importance of not dwelling either in the samsaric condition or in the peaceful bliss of nirvana. This perspective is distinct from the early Buddhist view of nirvana, which is seen by Mahayana practitioners as quietist and too removed from the world; the other extreme is to be immersed in the preoccupations of the samsaric condition, which is to dwell in delusion. The sutric and tantric followers of the Mahayana tradition want to avoid these two extremes. Their understanding of nonabiding nirvana is that it means to be in the world but not of it.

Although the goal of Sutra and Tantra is the same, there is a great deal of difference in the methods used to achieve that goal. The tantric teachings offer methods not available in the sutric teachings, which are organized into levels of development. The tantric system uses techniques not found in the sutric teachings, such as visualization, recitation of mantras, and working with the physical energies of the body. Sutrayana is studied through books and teachings where one comes across concepts like Buddha-nature and emptiness. A better understanding of these would help us to understand Tantra also. The notions of karmic propensities, the five poisons, and the four levels of consciousness are all found in sutric literature.

Even the visualization of deities has to be understood from the sutric point of view. For example, a deity may have six legs in order to represent the six paramitas. All of these elements are symbols for certain spiritual qualities, which can be realized through certain deities. So we have to understand what the six paramitas are, and we find those paramitas described in detail in the Sutras.

Another example is the fifty-one skulls that some deities wear around their necks. These skulls are supposed to represent the fifty-one types of subconscious mental gossip, or what is normally translated as "mental events." You will actually find sutric teachings that list all fifty-one mental events, but of course you do not have to find out which skull represents which mental event! The deities have to be understood symbolically, and these symbols can be better grasped though having an understanding of the sutric conceptual categories to which they refer. If we do not understand these things symbolically, we could come very close to practicing demonology.

Tantric methods make it possible to deal with delusions and conflicting emotions directly. In fact, the delusions that are to be abandoned, and the different types of spiritual qualities that need to be cultivated, are seen as two sides of the same coin rather than two totally opposite kinds of experience. For this reason, the tantric system is also called the esoteric tradition, not because there is anything that needs to be kept secret particularly, but because to practice Tantrism requires certain attributes in the practitioner. In a sense, one needs to have some ability to practice Tantra; otherwise one would not derive any benefit from it despite one's practice. The tantric teachings are kept secret to a certain extent, not because their contents should not be revealed, but because many people are not able to comprehend them.

If one has the required abilities, it is possible to achieve the goal of enlightenment in a short time through the use of tantric methods. This is not the case with the sutric method. To put it another way, the difference between the sutric and tantric methods lies in their use of relative truth. The recitations of mantras, visualization of deities, and other practices are all ways of exploiting the nature of relative truth, because they enable the practitioner to come into contact with relative truth directly. However, the absolute truth that is realized by the methods of Tantra is the same truth that is discussed in the sutric teachings.

The tantric system has many different names, such as Tantrayana, Vajrayana, and Mantrayana. Tantra is called *gyü* in Tibetan, meaning "continuity," because the tantric teachings emphasize the idea of continuity between the inner nature of a person in the condition of samsara and the inner nature of that same person when in the state of nirvana. When people become enlightened they do not discover themselves to be a totally different entity, because Buddha-nature has been there right from the beginning. Tantrism stresses the importance of Buddha-nature. The word *vajrayana*, or the "vehicle of the vajra," actually has the same connotation. *Vajra* means "indestructibility," and so the vajra is the symbol of indestructibility, which again refers to the quality of the Buddha-nature. For example, the practice of *vajrasattva* (a form of tantric purification using visualization of the deity Vajrasattva and recitation of mantra) is the practice of Buddha-nature. *Sattva* means "mind," so *vajrasattva* refers to the "indestructible mind," which is Buddha-nature, or the nature of mind. Vajrayana also emphasizes the importance of this concept of Buddha-nature.

While most sutric teachings portray samsara as being the opposite of nirvana, the tantric emphasis on Buddha-nature brings the concepts of samsara and nirvana together. While the sutras teach that everything samsaric is to be abandoned and everything displaying the qualities of nirvana is to be cultivated, in the tantric understanding Buddha-nature underlies all of one's samsaric and nirvanic experiences. This is why the concepts of indestructibility and continuity are emphasized in Tantra in relation to the understanding of Buddha-nature.

SEX IN TANTRA

Tantrism deals with our experiences directly. The peaceful deities, visualized as being seductive and alluring, can help us deal with desire, while visualizing wrathful deities can help us to transform aggression. Defilements and delusions need not be abandoned in Tantra, for they can be made use of on the path. In a tantric context, sometimes even sex has been used. But there is a great deal of confusion regarding this. Those who want to sanitize Tantrism say that it does not make use of sex at all, while others make it seem as if Tantra is nothing but sex! As usual, the truth lies somewhere in between. Even recent scholars such as Lobsang Lhalungpa, the translator of *Moonbeams of Mahamudra* and other texts, says there is no room for sex in Tantra. On the other hand, Jeffrey Hopkins, a follower of the Geluk tradition, which normally does not discuss this aspect of Tantra, mentions that the use of sex has not been discarded altogether even within his tradition.

If we are to understand the role of sex within Tantrism, we need to consider the context of the three mudras: *Karmamudra, Jnanamudra*, and *Mahamudra*. Karmamudra is the yogic practice of sex in order to generate bliss. The idea is that sexual methods make it possible to overcome the sense of duality and therefore experience bliss, with sexual desire transformed into what is called *mahasukha*, or "great bliss." However, the same effect can be obtained through the practice of Jnanamudra, which means "deities in union." You may have seen such deities in Tibetan paintings. They are visualized in the act of sexual union in order to obtain the same goal and experience the same bliss that the practice of Karmamudra generates. But the bliss experienced on both of these levels is said to be incomparable to the bliss that one can experience through the practice of Mahamudra. So even if one uses sexual methods, there is nothing wonderful about them—they are just methods.

LEVELS OF TANTRA

Vajrayana practices, or tantric teachings, have been systematized into four categories, and practitioners are encouraged to follow the tantric teachings in a systematic and gradual way. The relationship that exists between the visualized deities and the practitioner will go through different transitions, depending upon the level of Tantra with which the person engages. Even the natures of the visualized deities are different; they may be wrathful or peaceful, for example.

Kriya Tantra

The first level of Tantra is Kriya Tantra, or *bya gyü* in Tibetan. The practice of Kriya Tantra emphasizes rituals, which are very important to observe precisely and clearly. For instance, it is important to observe cleanliness. People who practice Kriya Tantra are supposed to engage in ritual bathing and wash their bodies five or six times a day. They must also stick to a strict vegetarian diet. The deities who are visualized are mostly peaceful, and the relationship between the deity and the practitioner is one in which the practitioner plays a subservient role. The practitioner sees the deity as the master and him- or herself as the servant.

In Tantrism we have hundreds and even thousands of deities, but they all belong to what are known as Buddha families. Three different Buddha families are mentioned on the level of Kriya Tantra: the Padma, or Lotus family; the Vajra family; and the family of the Buddhas. Of course, all the Buddhas are included in the Buddha family. The principal deity of the Lotus family is Avalokiteshvara, and the principle deity of the Vajra family is Vajrapani.

In order to practice the visualizations and engage in the *sadhana* or practice of Tantra, one needs to receive the proper empowerment, or *abhisheka*. According to Jamgön Kongtrül the Great, the Sanskrit word *abhisheka* derives from two different sources. The first is *abhi-*

kensa, which means "sprinkling." This is part of every single empowerment that we receive and symbolizes the purification of the defilements. The other word is *abikenta*, which means "putting something into a container." Jamgön Kongtrül says this means that when the mind has become cleansed of the defilements, the qualities of wisdom can be put into it, and that therefore the real connotation of *abhisheka* is empowerment. It is through receiving the empowerment that one's practice becomes effective. Jamgön Kongtrül says it is therefore extremely important that we abide by the proper procedure for imparting and receiving these empowerments. It should be done very precisely, because without empowerment one's practice cannot be effective. Through the imparting and receiving of empowerment, a certain kind of relationship is established between the teacher and the student. This relationship becomes transformed at that point, and from then onward it is no longer ordinary or insignificant. Jamgön Kongtrül says that it is comparable to marriage vows. Just as the relationship between two people can be transformed through a marriage ceremony to mean something different from what it meant in the past, so too can the relationship between teacher and disciple be transformed.

There are two different types of empowerments on the level of Kriya Tantra. The first is the empowerment of sprinkling water, and the second is the empowerment of the crown. The empowerment of sprinkling water uses a vase, and the empowerment of the crown is conferred with the mudra of the crown rather than with an actual crown itself. The deities visualized within the context of Kriya Tantra consist of two different types, because they can be visualized in either a full or a symbolic form. Instead of visualizing a deity with the hands, face, and feet of a fully developed body, one can visualize the deity symbolically—as a vajra, for instance. The deity can also be visualized in the form of a letter of the Tibetan alphabet. For example, one can visualize the heart syllable, which is considered to be the same as visualizing the deity itself. However, at the Kriya Tantra level, the relationship between the practitioner and the deity is essentially one of inequality. We see ourselves as being deluded, while the deity is worshiped as having all the power to impart to us.

Charya Tantra

The practitioner then proceeds to the next stage, which is Charya Tantra, or *chö gyü*. Charya Tantra emphasizes the importance of both meditative states and ritual observances. *Charya* means "ritual practice" and deals with physical postures and the recitation of mantras, but it also involves the mental aspect of meditation, which is developed through visualization practices. When one practices the visualization of deities on the level of Charya Tantra, it is no longer based upon the same sense of inequality that defined Kriya Tantra. The deities are seen more as friends than exalted beings to be worshiped, even while having nothing in common with the practitioner in terms of qualities. When it is said in the tantric teachings, that we visualize ourselves as a deity, it says that we should also develop something, which is called "divine pride." This means that we should develop confidence, rather than pride in the conventional sense. Everything that we are looking for is already inside us, if we only knew how to tap into these resources.

The deities are also classified in three Buddha families on the level of Charya Tantra, known as the families of body, speech, and mind. Except for the names, there seems to be no difference between the actual deities belonging to these Buddha families in Kriya and Charya Tantra. There is a slight difference with regard to the empowerments, because there are five empowerments instead of two. When a student is ready to practice Charya Tantra, he or she needs to receive these five empowerments, which consist of the empowerment of sprinkling water, the crown, the vajra, the bell, and the name.

In Charya Tantra the deities are visualized as having two aspects, relative and absolute. Sometimes the absolute aspect of the deity is called the purity aspect of the deity, while the relative aspect or impure aspect is the actual visualization of the deity itself. The absolute nature of the visualized deities is understood to be no different from one's own Buddha-nature, or the nature of mind. The basic point is that the visualization of the deities is not absolute, because the deities are a projection of the mind.

Anuyoga Tantra

From Charya Tantra one moves onto the next level, which is Anu-yoga Tantra, or *jesu naljor gyü*. On this level, one relies less and less on relative truth and aims more toward absolute truth. As with Charya Tantra, one needs to receive five empowerments to practice the Anuyoga Tantras. These are the empowerment of sprinkling water, the crown, the vajra, the bell, and the flower. On the Anuyoga tantric level, it is said that one must have developed bodhichitta and taken the Bodhisattva vow, for without it one cannot continue the practice. Anuyoga Tantra practice involves dealing with delusions and defilements directly, so that they can become transformed into the five wisdoms. The five Buddha families are actually the symbolic representations of these five wisdoms.

In the Mahayana teachings, particularly those belonging to the last turning of the Wheel of Dharma, five levels of consciousness are discussed. The first level is *alayavijnana,* or "storehouse conscious-ness." This storehouse consciousness retains all the karmic propensi-ties. In some ways it is comparable to the unconscious as this is understood in the West. These karmic propensities or tendencies are called *pagchak* in Tibetan, and *varsana* in Sanskrit. *Pakchak* literally means "existing in a hidden way," or not immediately conscious. So these *pakchak,* or karmic traces and dispositions, operate on the level of the storehouse consciousness, and the storehouse consciousness be-comes transformed into what is called *mirrorlike wisdom.*

The second level of consciousness is called the ego-mind, which is *nyön yid* in Tibetan, or *manovijnana* in Sanskrit. Because of these karmic propensities, the experiences of our senses are filtered through the ego-mind, or our own subjective viewpoint in relation to how the ego views the world. The ego-mind is seen as the seat of the notion of the self, and any kind of self-centeredness or egocentricity arising from this notion. This ego-mind becomes transformed into the *wis-dom of equanimity.*

The next level of consciousness is what we normally mean by consciousness, the mind that thinks, feels, and experiences at a con-scious level on a moment-by-moment basis. This is transformed into *discriminating wisdom.*

Lastly, the five sense consciousnesses, or five sensory impressions that give us information about the external world, become transformed through the process of Anuyoga Tantra into *all-accomplishing wisdom*.

All this is made possible because of the fifth wisdom, called the *wisdom of dharmadhatu,* or the *wisdom of dharmakaya*, which is nothing other than Buddha-nature itself. Buddha-nature is the basis of both the samsaric and nirvanic experience. Therefore, the realization of Buddha-nature manifests as this wisdom of dharmadhatu (ultimate reality) or dharmakaya. Through the practice of Anuyoga Tantra, one uses these techniques to deal with delusions directly.

When understood properly, these very delusions can be transformed into wisdom, and therefore the delusions are the very material that constitutes what we mean by wisdom. That at least is the tantric understanding, which is likened to the alchemic process of turning lead into gold. One does not make a sharp distinction between what should be abandoned and what should be cultivated. If one knows how to deal with things that normally give rise to delusions, one can in fact give rise to insight and wisdom instead.

Sometimes, tantric practitioners are compared to peacocks, not because of their arrogance but because of the Indian myth that peacocks live on poison. Just as the peacock is able to use poison as food, a capable tantric practitioner should be able to take the five poisons of attachment, anger, jealousy, pride, and ignorance, and transform them into the five wisdoms.

Generally speaking, human beings have five poisons, but usually one poison will predominate. One may have anger as the main problem, or pride, or jealousy. The five poisons correspond to the five Buddha families. For example, the Buddha of the Padma family, which is red in color, represents the transformed energy of desire. There is a positive spiritual potential corresponding to each particular poison, and this can be developed through working with the energy of that poison. Of course, not everybody belongs to the same Buddha family, but still one would need to engage in the types of practices associated with all the Buddha families. However, the teacher may recommend that one do a particular practice because one needs to work with a particular poison. Another way of explaining it is the transformation of what we call the five psychophysical constituents, or the five *skandhas*, into the five wisdoms. There is nothing that one needs to abandon; rather, one can make use of everything in order to achieve enlightenment.

The final level of Tantra is Mahanuttarayoga Tantra, which is the "supreme yoga," and this we shall discuss in the next chapter.

14

SUPREME YOGA TANTRA

Becoming a Total Person

THE FINAL LEVEL OF TANTRA, Mahanuttarayoga Tantra, or *la-me chenpo'i gyü*, is considered to be the supreme level. It is also the most difficult one to practice. Unlike the other Tantras, on this level the practitioner deals directly with his or her conflicting emotions through practices such as the visualization of wrathful deities. In Mahanuttarayoga Tantra effort is made constantly to look at what is frightening, what is intimidating, what produces sexual desire, and so on, and to attempt to link these experiences with more liberating spiritual experiences, in order to see these very energies as expressions of wisdom. For that reason, one visualizes deities in sexual union and the like.

Visualizing wrathful deities stirs up emotions more than visualizing peaceful deities. These wrathful deities can be very intimidating. They are usually adorned with skulls and wear animal skins and things of that nature. However, all this must be understood symbolically, and one needs to understand what these symbols represent in each specific practice. The deities have a certain number of heads or a certain number of limbs for a specific reason, and the same applies to the animal skins or hides that they wear. Human skin, for example, can represent desire; a tiger skin can represent hatred; an elephant skin can represent ignorance. I'm simply giving these as examples, because these symbolic meanings are not fixed in relation to particular images. They vary from practice to practice and from deity to deity, so that one has to understand the symbolic meaning in each particular context. In all these practices, the emphasis is upon bringing about some kind of marriage between the sacred and the profane. With that understanding, one takes the necessary empowerments in the Mahanuttarayoga Tantra, as with the previous Tantras. The first empowerment is the *vase empowerment*, and the first part of this consists of the empowerment of sprinkling water, which symbolizes the purification of the defilements. Then the empowerment of the crown is given; according to Mahanuttarayoga Tantra, the significance of this empowerment is that the practitioner has to find out to which Buddha family he or she belongs. The crown of that particular Buddha family is then placed on the head of the practitioner, in a symbolic way. The other part of the vase empowerment consists of placing a vajra on the practitioner's head, to symbolize the inseparability of emptiness and compassion. In addition to all this, a new name is given to the practitioner, which symbolizes the fact that the practitioner is being "reborn." These empowerments are all considered a part of the vase empowerment.

This is followed by the *secret empowerment*, which is called secret mainly because it empowers one to practice the visualization of deities in union. The significance of union, of course, is the coming together of the dualities of subject and object, or wisdom and emptiness, or compassion and wisdom. To symbolize the experience of bliss that is the result of this union, one is given medicinal blessing pills as part of the empowerment. The mandala associated with the vase empowerment is the external mandala, constructed of sand or painted on canvas. The mandala of the secret empowerment is not physical at all, but mental. This is because the vase empowerment is received in order to eradicate the defilements of the physical body, whereas the secret empowerment is intended to eradicate the defilements of speech.

The third empowerment is the *empowerment of wisdom,* which

enables the practitioner to engage in such practices as tummo, or "mystic heat yoga." The main point here is to transform the sexual energy through these practices. The way that this is achieved depends upon the practitioner, or upon whether he or she is a monk or nun, celibate or noncelibate. In any case, the basic aim is to realize great bliss through the transformation of sexual energies. In the practice of mystic heat, for example, even as practiced by celibates, the mystic heat is made to rise from the navel center up through the central channel, until it melts what is called the bodhichitta or "life essence," and then it descends again. As the life essence descends through the central channel, one experiences different types of bliss at different levels. When practiced with a partner it is called karma yoga, and when practiced by celibate people it is called *jnana* or wisdom yoga. In either approach, the same objective is attained.

The final empowerment is called the *empowerment of logos*, or word. Through the transformation of sexual energy one attains the experience of bliss, and through the experience of bliss it becomes easier to overcome the duality of subject and object. As this experience of bliss becomes more refined it is transformed into what is called great bliss, or *mahasukha*. (Sometimes it is also called co-emergent bliss). This great bliss coincides with the realization of the nature of mind, or the realization of Mahamudra. From this perspective of Mahamudra, the nature of mind has three aspects—bliss, emptiness, and nonconceptuality.

The fourth empowerment is essentially symbolic, because it does not empower the person to do any particular practice. The empowerment of the logos or word is a symbolic gesture pointing out the nature of the mind. The culmination of the practice has to do with transcending any subtle forms of attachment that may remain in relation to the blissful experiences associated with the practices of the third empowerment. One also realizes that the deities that one has visualized, the mantras recited, and the other practices undertaken, were just expedient methods, and that all these deities actually represent nothing other than the spiritual qualities that are already innate in the mind itself. So there is total transcendence of all conceptual fabrications.

In this way, the four levels of Tantra lead the practitioner through different stages of self-realization. Unlike the methods of the Sutrayana, Tantrism uses emotional conflicts as well as concepts in order to go beyond delusion. The way the concepts are used is through the practice of visualization, and as one becomes more acquainted with these visualizations they become more and more complex and demanding. Instead of abandoning concepts, however, one uses them. At the same time, one uses the conflicting emotions in order to transform them into their corresponding wisdoms. As with all other Buddhist practices, it is said that we must approach these practices step by step. We must prepare ourselves for these practices or else some of the more advanced stages can be overwhelming or disturbing to the mind rather than helpful.

It should be emphasized that we need to have proper guidance to practice these tantric methods. Because Tantrism is so expedient and so effective, if we miss the point with Tantra, its methods would do far more damage than a misunderstanding of the sutric methods would incur. However, if we do the practices properly and go through the various stages before undertaking the practices of the Mahanuttarayoga Tantra, then our efforts will be helpful not only in this life but also in the intermediate state after death. All the frightening beings that are described in the *Tibetan Book of the Dead* (*Bardo thödröl*), for example, are the same as the deities visualized in the Mahanuttarayoga Tantras. That does not mean that the deities we encounter in the intermediary state would be exactly like the deities we might have visualized. But through repeated use of visualizations, we remind ourselves of the fact that these deities are the product of our imagination rather than something real, possessed of independent existence. This realization could help us at the time of death.

As the teachings point out, just because we know that the frightening experiences that occur in sleep or dreams are only mental illusions does not mean that we have the capacity to control them while we are actually experiencing these things. However, through the practice of dream yoga—which is a part of the Mahanuttarayoga Tantra practices—it is possible to have control over our dreams right now. We can have lucid dreams and actually realize that it is all a dream while we are dreaming; therefore, if we are having frightening experiences at the time, there is nothing to be frightened of.

In a similar way, the practices of deity visualization are helpful for realizing the nature of the mind. If this is realized, we would be able to recognize what is going on even during the experiences of the intermediary state. During the practice of Mahanuttarayoga Tantra we visualize the most frightening deities we can imagine, in order to acquaint ourselves with the dark side of our own consciousness. The most frightening, most grotesque, most revolting beings are realized, all with the symbolic meaning of spiritual qualities.

When we say that the deities are projections of the mind, that does not mean that the deities do not have a certain kind of power in themselves. I think that kind of interpretation comes from the Western understanding that everything external to the mind is more real than anything in the mind. But this is not necessarily the case. For example, the delusions of a psychotic are only in his or her mind, but those delusions have a very powerful influence on that person. This is also true with the use of visualizations, which can be very powerful images for the mind, in this particular case with the healing process. In Buddhist terms it is expressed this way: from the ultimate point of view the deity is a projection of the mind, but from the relative point of view, because the deities are projected outward, they do have some kind of existence of their own. Therefore, they can have some influence on the mind of the practitioner on the relative level. We should not think that because everything is mental there is no point in doing any of this, that it is all a waste of time.

The aim of tantric practice is to bridge the gap between the conscious and the unconscious, the sacred and the profane, and all other dualities. Only when we do this can we appreciate the purpose of visualizing deities ripping flesh with their teeth, feasting on a human heart, drinking blood, and things of that nature. It provides a method for becoming a total person, because we are able to acknowledge all that is undesirable and disturbing. That, I think, is what becoming an enlightened person is all about.

15

THE SIX YOGAS OF NAROPA

Dealing with Conflicting Emotions

THE SIX YOGAS were given to the Indian siddha Naropa as an adjunct to his daily Mahamudra meditation. These yogas consists of mystic heat, illusory body, dream, clear light, bardo, and transference of consciousness. The Six Yogas are designed to help practitioners deal with conflicting emotions of various kinds. It would not be appropriate to talk about the Six Yogas in detail here because for that one would need to have taken the necessary empowerments and completed the preliminary practices. However, I can explain the nature of these practices and the reasons why a practitioner may choose to engage in them. Before embarking on the practice of the Six Yogas, it is essential to complete both the common and uncommon preliminary practices. The common preliminaries consist of contemplation of impermanence, karmic cause and effect, precious human rebirth, and the sufferings of samsara. The uncommon preliminary practices include prostration, vajrasattva, mandala, and guru yoga.

Having successfully completed the required preliminary practices, the yogi or yogini can embark upon the Six Yogas of Naropa. According to the traditional teachings, mystic heat yoga is most suitable for individuals with immense energy and dedication. Dream yoga and the yoga of clear light, on the other hand, would be the most appropriate for someone who has a lethargic disposition. The yogas are practiced in relation to one's own predilections, habit patterns, and psychological makeup. The practice of mystic heat, for example, is an effective tool for working with sexual lust, whereas illusory body yoga is recommended for people with aggressive tendencies. For those who are disposed toward mental obscurations and defilements, the yoga of clear light is used as an antidote. Bardo yoga is practiced in order to prepare ourselves for our inevitable demise and postmortem state of bardo. Transference of consciousness is practiced because of the separation of body and mind at the time of death. Through this practice, it is possible to become familiar with that experience of transference of consciousness while one is alive.

In and through the practice of these Six Yogas, the yogi or yogini is able to generate the experience of great bliss (*mahasukha*). Ordinarily we experience our desires as the source of attachment and fixation. But through practice, it is possible to transform what is base and constricting into something that is sublime and liberating. Then the psychophysical energy pathways (*nadis*), psychophysical energy current (*prana*), psychophysical energy center (*chakra*) and life essence (*bindi*) begin to function at their optimum level, thus affording the practitioner a hitherto unknown strata of psychosomatic health and vigor. The six doctrines of Naropa therefore represent the most efficient way of deploying skillful means (*upaya*) in tantric practice, precisely because each yoga is designed to deal with a particular type of emotional conflict (*klesha*).

MYSTIC HEAT YOGA (*Tummo*)

In order to transform sexuality into spirituality, mystic heat is practiced. Here, ordinary bodily and sexual pleasure is transformed into great bliss. This experience of bliss leads to the realization of the ultimate reality, or emptiness. The spiritual experience of bliss is inseparable from emptiness. This is accomplished through training the energy pathways, psychophysical energy, and life essence. There are three main energy pathways, one in the center, one on the right, and one on the left. The right and left energy pathways represent the male and female elements. There are also five psychophysical energy centers stationed at specific points in the body. The crown chakra is stationed in the head region and is known as the chakra of bliss. The chakra of pure indulgence is stationed at the throat center. At the heart rests the chakra of mental effusion. At the navel rests the chakra of creative manifestations and at the genitals lies the chakra of pleasure.

The crown chakra is referred to as the center of bliss. Even during ordinary sexual intercourse—according to tantric medicospiritual systems—bliss descends from the crown region. The throat chakra has earned the name of pure indulgence because we ingest food and drink through this aperture. The heart chakra is referred to as the center of mental effusion because it is from here that feelings such as attraction and aversion emanate. The navel chakra is known as the center of creative manifestations because herein lies the creative life force. Even the warmth of the body is supposed to flow to its extremities from this region, considered to be the creative source of the life force itself. The genital chakra is known as the center of pleasure. In the teachings it is said that in normal circumstances the experience of pleasure descends from the crown center, through the throat center and navel center to the genital center where the sexual energy is released. However, through tantric practice, the sexual energy is deliberately retained and reversed rather than released. The practitioner does not lose control. This reversal of the sexual energy is what produces great bliss. This kind of self-control takes a great deal of practice, of course.

The yogi or yogini transforms the ordinary energy pathways into their purer and more liberating counterparts. The mystic heat is practiced to generate heat, and from heat, bliss is produced. It is also said that apart from the spiritual realizations that may result from this practice, one can also expect to enjoy a tremendous sense of well-being, brought about by equalizing the elements. Also, as a result of having practiced mystic heat, one is no longer affected by extreme elements of heat or cold.

Illusory Body Yoga

The practice of illusory body yoga enables us to work with our aggression. Through this practice we can realize the nonsubstantial nature of aggression and thereby realize the illusory nature of things. There are several ways to contemplate illusion. The first is to contemplate *physical objects*, the second is contemplation of *speech*, and the third is contemplation of *mental cogitation*. Contemplation of physical objects means regarding them as similar to dreams. When we are dreaming we may have the feeling that we have met so-and-so, lived in such-and-such a house, and so on. Upon awakening we realize that what we dreamed about was all illusory. Likewise, everything that looks solid and impenetrable in the phenomenal world is in reality non-substantial and devoid of essence. This is what is realized through this yoga.

Dream Yoga

Dream yoga practice has the benefit of producing lucid dreaming so that we can become conscious of our dreams while we are still asleep. In that way, even dream experiences can be used to foster our spiritual progress, and no time is wasted during both waking and sleeping hours. This practice has two components, the recognition of dreams as dreams and the realization of dreams as illusory. By becoming familiar with these two components of dream yoga, the yogi or yogini develops the capacity to transform dreams at will. Thus, a nightmare may be transformed into a pleasant dream. Except for dreams that are portents of future events and the like, most dreams are seen to be the product of our karmic inheritance and its habitual tendencies. There is an inextricable relationship between deity yoga (visualization of deities) and the practice of dream yoga at night. Both deal with mental images, which are very important for understanding how the mind's many permutations work.

Clear Light Yoga

As the yogi or yogini becomes more proficient in dream yoga, he or she is able to maintain awareness during dream experiences, without yielding to the powerful pull of stupor and sloth. Through clear light yoga, the yogi or yogini develops immense mental perspicacity and clarity as a result of the diminishing influence of ignorance.

So practitioners of the Six Yogas do the mystic heat and illusory body yogas during the day, and meditate on dream yoga and the yoga of clear light at night. Mystic heat and illusory body yogas, as already mentioned, act as antidotes for excessive desire and aggression. Dream yoga is formulated to dispel mental stupor and heaviness. We supplement this practice with the yoga of clear light. The result of these practices is mental clarity and perspicacity, so that the yogi or yogini is able to maintain a sense of awareness both day and night. It is through these practices that we are able to transform the five poisons and realize Mahamudra. Six Yogas are the method, and the Mahamudra is the goal.

BARDO YOGA

The practice of bardo yoga has four divisions: the natural bardo of this life, the painful bardo of dying, the luminous bardo of dharmata, and the karmic bardo of becoming.

Bardo simply means "in-between." The natural bardo of this life includes everything from the moment of birth to the time of death. Thus, this life is sandwiched in between birth and death. According to Buddhism, life itself consists of a continuous series of birth, death, and rebirth. In this sense, the emergence of a fresh thought, a new life situation, or a novel experience also represents birth. When these fade into only faint memories, or into the unconscious, that is death. The reemergence of similar life/mind experiences represents rebirth. We therefore have to accustom ourselves to our own mortality in the natural bardo of this life. If we succeed in doing that, then we have already prepared ourselves for the painful bardo of dying.

The Painful Bardo of Dying

The painful bardo of dying has two divisions. These are the dissolution of the sense faculties, sense organs, and outer elements (*jung wa*), and the dissolution of inner mental events (*sem jung*). According to the tantric medical system, life is initially formed through the coming together of the five elements. These same elements sustain the life thus acquired. They are also responsible for the cause of death. The harmonious functioning among the elements is therefore essential for the perpetuation of life. When the elements stop functioning together, this signals the advent of the painful bardo of dying.

Along with the dissolution of the elements is the gradual withdrawal of psychophysical energy from the body. As a result, the dying person experiences difficulties with normal bodily functions. The first thing to go is the body's ability to digest food. They are no longer able to take normal food or drink and start to labor with breathing. They can no longer move their limbs at will, and they lose voluntary control over their bowels. The mind becomes delirious and confused.

Also included in the inventory of the dying person's afflictions and woes is the dissolution of the five elements. The earth element provides the body with its solidity and strength. At the time of death, however, this element dissolves into water, which results in progressive weakening of the body. The neck cannot support the head, the legs can't hold the body upright, and so on. Apart from these obvious physical signs of approaching death, there are corresponding mental signs. The mind becomes dull, opaque, and confused.

Then the water element dissolves into the fire element. Since the water element supplies the body with its much-needed fluid, the dissolution of this element not unexpectedly leads to dryness of the mouth and tongue. The tongue also becomes stiff. Mentally the dying person becomes agitated and anxious.

This is followed by the dissolution of the fire element into the wind element. Physical signs include a chilling of the mouth and nose as the heat of the body vanishes at this point. One's mind slips in and out of consciousness and has difficulties in recognizing or identifying things.

This gradual and painful process of dissolution culminates in the wind element dissolving into consciousness. The dying individual begins to breath erratically, with long exhalations and difficult inhalations. Mentally he or she begins to hallucinate. The nature of these hallucinations is determined by one's life experiences and karmic inheritance. The sense faculties and sensory apparatus cease to function, so that he is no longer capable of apprehending sensory objects at all, or at best misapprehends them.

When the senses have ceased to function altogether, the consciousness dissolves into the element of space, at which point the dying person stops breathing. It is mentioned in the literature on the death and dying process that there is still some lingering warmth remaining in the heart region at this point. It is also said that in certain rare circumstances the dying person may be revived and brought back to life. Apart from these unusual exceptions, this is where the demarcation line between life and death is drawn. Consciousness is wrenched from the body through the force of one's karma, and the process of dissolution of gross and subtle thoughts comes into effect. At the onset of this fading of thoughts, the deceased begins to perceive apparitions of whiteness, redness, and blackness.

The tantric literature explicates two types of life energy sources. These are known as life essence and reside in two different locales. One type of energy source is the male life essence, inherited from one's father and located in the cortex. The female energy source is inherited from one's mother and dwells in the navel region. The male essence is white, while the female essence is red. At the time of death, owing to the movement of the psychophysical energy, the male life essence that is located in the crown area is forced to move downwards through the central energy pathway, which then produces the perception of whiteness in the deceased. A whiteness comparable to the moonlight is said to appear. Then there is an upward movement of the female life essence, which resides in the navel region. This produces apparitions of redness comparable to the hue of the sun's radiance. Through the collision of these two types of life essence at the heart chakra, the dying person experiences blackout and is now dead, a disembodied being.

The Luminous Bardo of Dharmata

The apparitions of the white and red lights are referred to as phenomenal luminosity, while the experience of clear light at this juncture in the postmortem state is known as ground or ultimate luminosity. These two forms of luminosity are present in the mind itself in the form of Buddha-nature. As all the defiling factors of the mind have ceased for a very short time, the deceased is provided with the opportunity to recognize his or her innate nature. The Buddha-nature is present in everyone, so that we cannot extricate ourselves from it, yet that does not mean that we can recognize it when the time comes. It is for this reason that practices like the Six Yogas are undertaken.

The cultivation of insight into the nature of the mind is known as *son luminosity,* and what is innately present in the mind is known as *mother luminosity.* If the deceased is able to seize this precious moment and realize that the experience of luminosity in that situation is the same as knowing one's own nature, then there is release from samsaric bondage. Failure to recognize one's own nature in this instance would lead to all forms of mental anguish. Visions of beings with wrathful appearance, with multiple heads and multiple limbs, make their appearance in the bardo. It is not only frightful apparitions that terrorize the pitiful bardo being, however. The deceased is also subjected to the most frightening and dreadful sounds that one could possibly imagine.

After a period of enduring this agonizing mental torture, the deceased is mercifully rendered unconscious through the sheer intensity of the experience. All the previous manifestations disappear, and he finds himself in a radically different environment where the surroundings are translucent, iridescent, and imbued with light. This is a world populated by peaceful beings who are regal and beautifully adorned. This is followed by visions of spectacular displays of five-colored light.

There is one key point that the deceased has to pay attention to throughout the journey in the bardo, so as not to be taken in by the bardo apparitions: He must see that these apparitions are products of his own mind and therefore devoid of any objective reality. The tantric practice of visualization—which includes deities of both peaceful and wrathful nature—is seen as an extremely useful tool for acquainting ourselves with these various forms of mental projection. If we can recognize that the apparitions of the bardo are the product of the mind, then we can find liberation in the bardo itself. Otherwise we will be reborn, owing to our unresolved karmic history. Then the karmic bardo of becoming takes effect.

The Karmic Bardo of Becoming

Where and to whom we are born, and what sort of physical characteristics and mental propensities we have, are in large measure determined by our actions in the previous life and our attitudes at the time of death. Just as it is possible to reduce the pain of dying through spiritual practice, so too is it possible to lessen the trauma of birth by taking birth with consciousness and awareness. This is the way that highly advanced and realized beings are supposed to take birth.

TRANSFERENCE OF CONSCIOUSNESS

The yoga of transference of consciousness (*phowa*) involves transferring one's consciousness into a higher state. The idea is that through this training the yogi or yogini will be able to eject the consciousness through the crown chakra. Such a practitioner is able to exercise voluntary control over the mind-body system.

I hope that it has become clear to the reader that in Tantrism one can make use of a variety of situations and circumstances for the path, practiced in terms of either inner mental states or external environmental conditions, including our delusional states of mind. There is hardly anything that cannot be used to further one's spiritual powers if used correctly and if one is initiated into proper tantric method of practices. Of course, my description of the tantric path and its practices has been very general. To follow the tantric practices one must receive the authentic transmission from a guru whom one can trust. According to Tantrism, without the proper authorization and transmissions it is not possible for the initiate to prosper spiritually. In other words, such an individual will not realize the acquired siddhis of an enlightened being. By following the sutric approaches one can become an Arhat and Bodhisattva, and by following the tantric path one can realize the state of a tantrically realized being, or mahasiddha.

16

MAHAMUDRA AND THE
NATURE OF MIND
Going beyond Duality

THE CONCEPT OF MAHAMUDRA is very important in Tibetan Buddhism, particularly in the Kagyü tradition to which I belong. The word literally means "great seal" or "great symbol." *Mahamudra* basically refers to ultimate reality, to shunyata, or emptiness, but it also refers to the very nature of the mind. Ultimate reality, which is Mahamudra, is all-pervasive and nondifferentiated, neither subject nor object. That concept is not different from the nature of the mind itself.

From this point of view, the nature of the mind is different from the mind to which we normally refer in ordinary discourse. Usually, when people talk about the mind, they mean the mind that thinks, wills, and experiences emotions. When we talk about the nature of the mind, we are talking about something that goes beyond all that. Because the nature of the mind is indistinguishable from ultimate reality, which is emptiness, it no longer relates to the thinking process or the process of willing or the process of the experience of emotions. It goes beyond that. Therefore, the nature of the mind and ultimate reality are known as Mahamudra. There is that sense of non-duality.

In order to understand Mahamudra, we need to place it in the context of the Buddhist tradition generally.

From the point of view of Buddhism, the ultimate aim is to achieve nirvana or enlightenment. Nirvana is achieved as a result of having purified the mind, having overcome certain defilements and obscurations of the mind that afflict consciousness. As long as there are defilements such as anger, jealousy, and all kinds of egocentric tendencies, then sentient beings, including human beings, continue to experience a sense of dissatisfaction, frustration, and suffering.

These defilements exist in the first place because we generally have a very misguided way of understanding ourselves, of understanding the nature of what we consider our own self. We generally tend to think that the self is something immutable, lasting, and unchangeable. Based on this mental construct, we see everything from the point of view of a very stable, unchanging, permanent self. Of course, this can manifest in relation to various philosophical and religious ideas regarding the nature of the self and the notion of the soul, but it need not have anything to do with philosophy or religion.

Even if we do not believe in the immortality of the soul, almost all of us have the notion that it is "I" who feels happy, who feels sad, who experiences joy and unhappiness, and that there is something called the self that endures the varieties of experiences that we have. I may feel good or I may not feel good. I grow old. There is the feeling that there is some essential "I" that endures all these experiences. The experiencer who has the experiences is somehow more permanent than the experiences themselves.

When Buddhism talks about egolessness or selflessness, it does not mean that ego as such does not exist at all, as an empirical thing. Of course it does. However, our almost instinctive feeling that says there is something called ego with a permanent endurance is a simple mental construct; ego, like everything else, is impermanent. We must understand the self from the point of view of the Middle Way. A Buddhist does not deny the existence of the ego or of the self. The self exists on the relative level, but the self as an ultimate entity, as some kind of unchanging, permanent thing, does not exist. That does not mean that people do not have egos or that ego is totally illusory.

I think some people have interpreted the Buddhist notion of

selflessness or egolessness from that point of view. A Buddhist would say that the self is an aggregate, a *skandha*. We tend to think that the self is somehow distinguishable from our memories, emotions, thoughts, and attitudes. Somehow or other, the self remains at a distance, observing all these things going on or enduring these experiences. But Buddhists say that the self *is* the memories, thoughts, concepts, emotions, and attitudes. Put them together and you have a self. And if we take away all of that—in Buddhism we do this as an exercise—if we dissociate ourselves completely from our body, our memories, thoughts, emotions, attitudes, background and experiences, what remains? Nothing. We are something or somebody precisely because we have those things. They form an aggregate. Without them, we are nothing. That is emptiness.

It has been said that Western thought talks about the ego, while Buddhism teaches the nonexistence of ego. But even Western psychology does not make any reference to the concept of soul or any unchanging entity. So there are similarities there. Western psychology also talks about building up the ego, whereas Buddhism teaches how to break down the ego. But Buddhism also talks about building up self-confidence and feelings of self-worth. Buddhism does not say that, through the experience of egolessness, we should feel nothing, that we should feel bad about ourselves. Rather, through understanding the self to be impermanent, a real appreciation of it can be attained. The self is therefore something that can be transformed rather than something static.

As long as we do not have that understanding, we continue to grasp things, hold on to things, cling to things, because this tendency that human beings have, in terms of clinging to the self, automatically leads to clinging to other things, things outside the self. As long as human beings have the tendency to believe in a permanent self, then automatically we want to obliterate anything considered to be threatening to that notion of a self, or we want to pursue those things that we believe promote the solidification of that notion of a self. These are the two fundamental tendencies that develop from the notion of clinging to the self: aversion and excessive desire. Even aversions are a form of clinging. Clinging can manifest even in the form of clinging onto the idea of being resentful of someone, clinging to the notion of not being able to forgive, not being able to accept certain things, holding onto our feelings of hostility and resentment of other people. Desire can be either positive or negative, but clinging, grasping, and craving can never be positive. Clinging to anything, at least from a Buddhist point of view, is always unhealthy. But we must have desire to even be able to operate as human beings. Even from a spiritual point of view, unless we have the desire to sit on our cushion and meditate, we will never get anywhere. Unless we have the desire to attain enlightenment or become a Buddha we will never get anywhere. Unless we have desires, nothing can be achieved.

From the Buddhist point of view, there is nothing basically wrong with having the desire to have a good family, to want to look after our children, to want to have a good relationship, to want to have a good partner in life, to want to get a good job, or even to want to keep our job. The problem arises when those desires become exaggerated. When desires become transformed into forms of clinging and grasping and, at the same time, manifest in the form of craving, then it becomes a problem.

I think it is important to realize that Buddhism does not promote the idea of abandoning desires altogether. What Buddhism encourages is the idea that all forms of craving, grasping, and clinging, which are exaggerated forms of desire, have to be abandoned, because they ultimately cause suffering and unhappiness.

We may think that clinging or grasping would promote our happiness. Such misguided ideas come from having a mistaken notion about the self, from thinking that the self is a permanent, enduring entity, rather than realizing that the self—just like the experiences that the self endures—is impermanent and mutable, and therefore ephemeral. So, if we are to overcome the experience of suffering, then we must have proper insight into the nature of the mind, or into the nature of the self, because as long as we cling to this mistaken notion about the self we will experience varieties of suffering.

This is why meditation is so important. Through meditation, we become more aware of all this. As we become more and more aware of our tendencies, even without making any deliberate effort to drop certain habits, they will naturally drop away. In fact, if we try too hard to drop certain habits, they just become more solidified. Awareness is more important than actually making too much effort. If we try too hard to be nice, we end up not being nice! We become nice by becoming more aware of not being nice, rather than by trying too hard to be nice.

We must have a proper understanding of impermanence. A real appreciation of impermanence comes from realizing the impermanence of the self. What we regard as the self, which we think is unchanging and immutable, in fact is always in process. That could be seen as a good thing. Real transformation of the self can take place because the self is not some kind of immutable, unchanging entity. Otherwise, any kind of change or transformation in the self would only be apparent, not real, if the real self were something unchanging and permanent. The reason we need to gain proper insight into the nature of the self is precisely because real, lasting happiness comes from just that: having insight into the nature of the self, into the nature of the mind, and realizing the misconception of an unchangeable, permanent, enduring self.

All kinds of delusions and obscurations of the mind arise with this misconception, which in turn inhibit us from experiencing and perceiving reality. So, right from the beginning, Buddhism has emphasized the importance of purification of the mind, of how important it is to eradicate the defilements and obscurations of the mind and to gain proper self-knowledge, because that is the only way that real, lasting happiness can be attained. That same emphasis exists in the later Mahayana teachings, and also in the teachings of Mahamudra.

I have repeated some of these ideas because the teachings of Mahamudra make sense only in relation to understanding these fundamental Buddhist insights. Buddhism says that there are two veils: the veil of conceptual confusion and the veil of emotional conflict. Our thinking and our experience of emotions are intimately related; we cannot separate the two. Because of certain misconceptions regarding what we understand ourselves to be—for example, the notion that there is something called an enduring, permanent self—all kinds of emotional conflicts follow. When we change the conceptual structures of the mind, even emotions become transformed.

In the West, we have the notion that emotions and thoughts are very different and completely opposed to one another. From a Buddhist point of view, this is not true. What we believe in and how we think have a direct influence on the emotions we experience. Fundamentally, all our beliefs are tied up with our notion of the self. A Buddhist would say that our very dogmatic attitudes toward things or people—for example, toward people who belong to other religions or other races—reflect our own notion of the self. Things are seen either as threatening or as something that would help consolidate the notion of the self. But once that whole idea of the self as being an enduring, permanent entity is overcome, all the defiling tendencies of the mind subside, both on the conceptual as well as the emotional level.

The nature of the mind is not different from our thinking mind as such, yet they are not identical. Ignorance exists because we do not have insight into the nature of the mind. The nature of the mind is no different from the nature of the thoughts and emotions that we have; but because we do not have insight into the nature of the thoughts and emotions, we do not have insight into the nature of the mind.

How do we gain insight into the nature of the mind? Awareness is the key. When we meditate, we shouldn't think, "Why do I think about these trivial things? Why do certain emotions arise? Why do certain negative thoughts and emotions keep arising?" Not to judge them to be bad or terrible things that we have to get rid of, but simply to be aware of them is the Mahamudra approach. From the Mahamudra point of view, if we judge certain things to be bad or terrible, that is a form of clinging as well. We should just be aware of what arises in meditation.

The nature of the mind is said to be completely nondifferentiated and spacious, and is the source from which all of our experiences arise. It is not differentiated, in the sense that the nature of the mind, unlike our thoughts and emotions, does not exist as an entity.

Often it is compared to space. Space itself is not an entity, but it is because of space that clouds and other phenomena arise. Clouds have definable characteristics, whereas space itself has none. But space makes it possible for the clouds to be there in the first place. Sometimes the mind and its nature are compared to waves on the surface of the ocean and the ocean depths. One may perceive the waves, the activities on the surface of the ocean, but not actually realize the stillness and infinity of the depths of the ocean. Yet the nature of the waves and the nature of the depths of the ocean are the same thing, they are both water.

In a similar way, our thoughts and emotions have the same nature as the nature of the mind, but because of our ignorance, we cannot appreciate that. Psychologists and others try to understand the mind in relation to its definable characteristics, to thoughts and emotions. But there is another way of understanding the mind, which has to do with understanding the nature of the mind.

Maybe I should put it another way. From the Mahayana point of view, we talk about two levels of truth—the relative and the absolute. Absolute truth is emptiness. What that means is that things do not have enduring essence. There is no such thing as a substance that we can identify as being the essence of all things. On the other hand, this does not mean that things do not exist. The nature of all the chairs and tables that we perceive, for example, is emptiness. The problem is that we don't perceive the emptiness of the chairs and tables; we don't realize that they lack enduring essence. To realize that, we need to come to understand that emptiness does not exist over and above all these objects, but exists as their very nature. It is the same with the mind. We understand the nature of the mind through understanding the nature of our thoughts and emotions.

17

Mahamudra Meditation

*Allowing the Mind to Rest in
Its Natural State*

THE TEACHINGS OF MAHAMUDRA are drawn from two streams of
Mahayana thought, one being the Yogachara system and the other
the teachings of the Shunyavadins, who promoted the idea that ultimate reality is emptiness. Within the Buddhist tradition we say that
we need to eradicate certain defilements and obscurations of the mind
in order to realize ultimate truth or ultimate reality. The most effective way to achieve that goal is through the practice of meditation.

We have already discussed the two different types of Buddhist
meditation, shamatha and vipashyana. Conventionally, the meditation of tranquillity is presented in a way that suggests that, as the
mind becomes more focused, the meditator can enter into different
levels of concentration, or absorptions. As discursive thoughts subside, the mind attains different levels of absorption. Once we have
perfected shamatha, if we then engage in analytical vipashyana meditation, thinking no longer gives rise to conceptual confusions but produces insights.

Through shamatha, by focusing our mind on an external physical
object or the breath, we are able to practice mindfulness, and with

mindfulness comes awareness. When you are learning how to meditate, if you do not focus your mind on the breath or some kind of physical object but think, "I'll just be aware of what's going on in my mind," it doesn't work. That is why it is important to practice shamatha, so that stability is achieved. Then, when awareness develops from that stability and that mindfulness, the clarity aspect of the mind becomes manifest.

It is said that Buddhist meditation is different from other traditions only in relation to the practice of the meditation of insight. Other traditions also have techniques of quieting the mind, of helping the mind to become more focused. But it is through the practice of the meditation of insight that we realize there is no such thing as an enduring or permanent self and there is no enduring essence in physical and mental phenomena or in physical and mental properties.

Mahamudra also makes use of these two different techniques of shamatha and vipashyana, but it is not considered important to go through different levels of absorptions or concentrations. It is sufficient for us to have stabilized the mind. Even if we have not achieved any ultimate state of concentration, or have not managed to obtain any level of absorption, nonetheless the mind has become more stable and less susceptible to distractions. We can then proceed with the meditative practice of insight.

The meditative practice of insight according to Mahamudra is quite different from the conventional approaches. In the Mahayana tradition, one normally uses the analytical method to understand the lack of essence in all things, realizing that everything that exists in the physical and mental realm is a product of causes and conditions. This leads to a conceptual understanding of emptiness, which in turn leads to the direct experience of emptiness. But Mahamudra teachings say that if we were to focus on our mind itself and realize its nature, we would realize the nature of everything else.

The normal sutric approach of Mahayana uses external phenomena as objects of meditation, whereas Mahamudra uses the mind itself as the object of analytical meditation. But even in relation to the mind, Mahamudra does not analyze the mind in order to realize that it has the nature of emptiness. Rather, through contemplation, by allowing the mind to be in its natural state, the mind reveals itself to have that nature. So we do not need to have a conceptual grasp of the fact that the nature of the mind is empty. If the mind is allowed to be in its natural state and if all discursive thoughts subside, the nature of the mind itself is revealed as being empty of enduring essence.

In a normal context, when we engage in the practice of meditation we use different antidotes for different obstacles. According to Mahamudra, we should not be too concerned with the obstacles or with the use of the antidotes in order to quieten the mind. We should have a general sense that all obstacles that arise in meditation can be divided into two categories: stupor or drowsiness, and mental agitation.

With stupor, the mind is not disturbed by the agitation of discursive thoughts or emotional conflicts, but it has no sense of clarity. It becomes dull, and sometimes, of course, this is followed by sleepiness and drowsiness. Mental agitation is easier to detect, because our mind has fallen under the influence of discursive thoughts, distractions, emotional conflicts, and the like.

Instead of using different antidotes to control the mind in these situations, the Mahamudra approach recommends two methods: relaxation and a tightening-up process. If the mind has become dull, we should tighten it with the application of mindfulness. We should try to regenerate and refuel the sense of mindfulness of the meditation object, whatever it happens to be. If our mind is agitated, we should not apply too much mindfulness but should loosen the mind—in a sense, let go of mindfulness, or whatever it is that we are using in order to make the mind more focused.

This applies to our posture also. If our mind has become dull, we should straighten our spine, expand our chest, and tighten the body, though not too rigidly. If mental agitation is present, we should relax our posture so that we feel looser, and we should focus our mind on the lower part of the body.

The practice of mindfulness is called *trenpa* in Tibetan. It literally means "remembrance." Before awareness arises in meditation, the meditator has to learn how to focus the mind, which is achieved through the practice of mindfulness. We use a particular object in order to practice mindfulness. When mindfulness is practiced for a period of time, awareness arises as a product of mindfulness.

In Mahamudra teachings on shamatha, as beginners we first use some external object, such as a piece of wood, a pebble, or any kind of physical object in our visual field, and concentrate on that. Whenever the mind becomes distracted, through the use of mindfulness we remember to return to that object of meditation. After having done that for a period of time, we can use our own breath as the object of meditation. We apply mindfulness to the incoming and outgoing breath. In order to help with this process, we can even count the breaths, up to five, or up to eleven, or whatever sequence we choose. Each pair of breaths—outgoing and incoming—is counted as one. Counting helps the mind to be more focused on the object of meditation, which in this case is the breath. If we lose track of the counting when the mind wanders, we return to the beginning and start again.

When we have been able to do this with some success, then we move on to using the mind itself as the object of meditation. We try to be mindful of thoughts and emotions as they arise, without labeling them or judging them, but simply observing them. As this observation continues, mindfulness becomes transformed into awareness. So, if distraction arises, one becomes aware of that distraction; if dullness or stupor is present in the mind, one becomes aware of that; if mental agitation is present, one becomes aware of that. With the practice of meditation of tranquillity, the mind becomes more stabilized.

When we contemplate the mind itself and let the mind be in its natural state, then apart from mental stability, there must also be a sense of clarity. It is not sufficient that the mind has become stable; it is also important for clarity to be there. In Mahamudra teachings these aspects are described as *ne cha*, the aspect of stability, and *sal cha*, the aspect of clarity. A mind that is stable but without clarity is deficient. Both mental clarity as well as stability have to be present. If we pursue this, then even when thoughts and emotions arise, the stability and clarity of the mind are not disturbed.

To maintain mental clarity whether the mind is calm or agitated is the best form of meditation. Meditation does not mean that one's mind should always be calm or empty of thoughts and emotions. If a sense of mental stability or clarity is there even when the mind is in movement, that is the ultimate goal. For our aim is not to eradicate thoughts and emotions but to be able to maintain that sense of aware-ness, in movement as well as in a restful state. Mahamudra teachings use expressions like *ne gyu rik sum*. *Ne* means the mind when it is stable, when it's not agitated; *gyu* means the mind when it is in move-ment, when thoughts and emotions arise; *rik* means awareness, that sense of mental clarity; *sum* means three. So awareness is present whether the mind is in a state of rest or in a state of movement. It makes no difference.

When we achieve that, we realize the nature of the mind. Through awareness, we realize that the nature of the mind has the dual characteristic of being empty yet luminous. In terms of its emp-tiness, the nature of the mind is not different from nonmental things such as tables and chairs, because the nature of the table and of the chair is emptiness, and the nature of the mind is also emptiness. But in terms of the clarity aspect, the nature of the mind is different from non-mental things, because the nature of the mind is not only empty but luminous at the same time.

From this point of view, the nature of the mind is realized when the mind makes no distinction in meditation between mental agita-tion or a state of restfulness. Then the mind is left in its natural state and thoughts and emotions become self-liberated.

It is also said in Mahamudra teachings that we should not think of thoughts and emotions—particularly the negative ones—as being things we must eradicate. If we are able to realize the nature of these thoughts and emotions, we understand the nature of the mind itself. The teachings compare the relationship between the nature of the mind and the delusions to a lotus blossoming from mud, or to the manure used on a field. Just as a lotus blossoms in the mud, just as the farmer has to make use of smelly and repulsive manure in order to cultivate a field, similarly wisdom is attained not through eradica-tion of the defilements and obscurations of the mind but from real-ization of their very nature.

There is a Tibetan expression: *nyönmong pangwa gong rol na, yeshe gyawe ming yang me. Nyönmong* means "the obscurations of the mind"; *pangwa* means "to abandon"; *gong rol na* means "over and above"; *yeshe* means "wisdom"; *ming yang me* means "not even a name." Basically it translates as: "Having abandoned or eradicated the delusions and conceptual confusions of the mind, one cannot speak of wisdom. Wisdom is attained not from the eradication of the defilements but from understanding the nature of the defilements themselves."

That is why in Mahamudra teachings the phrase "ordinary mind" (*thamal gye shepa*) is used. Realizing the nature of the mind, or Buddha-nature, does not involve getting rid of anything that exists within the mind. It comes from realizing the nature of this very mind that we have: the mind that thinks, wills, anticipates, and feels. The problem lies not in having thoughts, feelings, and emotions, but in not understanding their nature. Through the practice of meditation, the mind becomes more stabilized and there is a sense of mental clarity. Then, when the mind is left to itself, if awareness is maintained as thoughts and emotions arise, those thoughts and emotions reveal the nature of the mind as much as the mind that is at rest.

From the Mahamudra point of view it is important not to try to force the mind to become more focused. We should simply use the very gentle methods of tightening and loosening, so that the mind can be in its natural state. If we try to use techniques of concentration, it is said that the mind is in fact not left in its natural state. We should allow the mind to be in its natural state, without any contrivances.

Pang lang dang drelwa is another phrase used in Mahamudra teachings. *Pang* means "to abandon"; *lang* means "to cultivate"; *dang drelwa* means "free from": "Free from any thought of cultivation of positive mental qualities or abandonment of negative thoughts and emotions." Our mind should be free from such concerns. As long as the mind is plagued by these tendencies of wanting to shun or abandon certain aspects of the mind that we find undesirable, and wanting to pursue and cultivate the more positive aspects of the mind, the mind is not left in its natural state and its nature becomes obscured by interference.

So the very simple technique of letting the mind be should be conducted with the use of either tightening or loosening the body and mind. Even these two different methods should not be done with extreme deliberation or effort. Another expression in Mahamudra teachings is "letting the mind be in its natural state effortlessly." That effortlessness comes from not judging, not thinking that the thoughts and emotions that arise have somehow disturbed the mind or upset the meditation; but realizing that as long as our mind is focused and there is a sense of awareness, no matter what arises in the mind— whether the mind is stable and at rest or in a state of movement with thoughts and emotions arising—we can realize the nature of the mind.

In this way, in the Mahamudra teachings tranquillity and insight are practiced together. The meditation of tranquillity is initially practiced in order to stabilize the mind. Then, gradually, by shifting our focus from meditation objects, such as external physical objects or the breath to the mind itself, the clarity aspect is developed. When we engage in meditation, these two aspects are present: the mind is stable and yet at the same time luminous. The mind is stable even when thoughts and emotions arise, insofar as awareness is not lost. Stability of the mind is judged not by whether the mind has thoughts and emotions, but by whether awareness is present. When that occurs, the third aspect of the nature of the mind—which is called bliss— becomes manifest.

Ultimately, the nature of the mind has three qualities. First, it is empty. Second, even though it is empty, it is luminous, unlike the emptiness of physical things or entities. Third, when our mind is stabilized and we can maintain awareness even when the mind is busy with thoughts and emotions, bliss is experienced. During meditation, when stability and clarity are established, bliss follows, because our mind is no longer disturbed even when thoughts and emotions arise. That is the bliss aspect. Obviously, it does not mean that we become "blissed out"!

According to Dzogchen teachings, or what is sometimes called Maha Ati in Sanskrit, the nature of the mind has the three aspects of emptiness, clarity, and "creativity." The nature of the mind may be empty and luminous, but that does not mean that thoughts and emotions cease to have any relevance. Doing meditation for a number of years does not mean that thoughts and emotions stop arising in the mind, but they no longer disturb the mind, which is seen as the creative aspect. In Dzogchen, it's called *tsal*, which means "creative" in terms of our experiences. Everything in the experience of samsara and nirvana comes from the creative aspect of the mind, in the sense of the mind being the producer of all kinds of experiences, both good and bad. As Saraha says: "The nature of the mind is king of all creators, because all our experiences of both samsara and nirvana arise from that." Everything is mind-dependent; even our perception of the external physical world is dependent on the mind.

The nature of the mind itself is called Mahamudra, because *mahamudra*, or "great seal," means that nothing exists outside of it. Everything is contained within Mahamudra itself, because the emptiness aspect is the same both in physical and mental phenomena. It is all-encompassing.

Four Yogas of Mahamudra

Because the Mahamudra path is understood as promoting the instantaneous path rather than the gradual path, it is often said that by remaining in one's natural state of mind one will realize Mahamudra in that instant. This sort of statement should be qualified by saying that a Mahamudra practitioner who has gained insight into the mind has not necessarily gained insight into final Buddhahood. The practitioner still has to be concerned about deepening that realization. As with most things in ordinary life, we may realize the importance of something, but that initial recognition is not sufficient to sustain us; with subsequent development, that initial recognition has to be cultivated, fostered, and worked with so that it can become mature as time goes by. For this reason the Mahamudra tradition includes the notion of the "four yogas": the yoga of one-pointedness, the yoga of nonconceptuality; the yoga of one taste, and the yoga of nonmeditation.

1. The yoga of one-pointedness is attained through the practice of *shi-ne* or shamatha, the meditation of tranquillity. As we all know, our mind is in a constant state of agitation—frantic, quick-to-judge, and impulsive in thought and behavior. Through this practice these mental states and behaviors become settled.

Our mind at the beginning is compared to a waterfall; we have no control, and we can't decide what we should believe in or choose which emotions to experience. They are seen as given, already present. Through tranquillity meditation, we become more aware of that state of being; with the practice of mindfulness, we begin to become more aware of ourselves, not only in terms of our beliefs, emotions, attitudes, and feelings, but also in terms of our behavior. These inner mental states get translated into our external physical behaviors. We can then observe what sort of mental states are beneficial for our growth and what sort of states are not beneficial; how they generate fear, anxiety, frustration, or feelings of self-worthlessness.

By becoming aware of such mental states and behavior, we are able to exercise more control and are not at the mercy of our feelings, emotions, thoughts, and attitudes. The mind then becomes more stable and relaxed as we learn to be more flexible, receptive, and generally less paranoid. The samsaric mind is a paranoid state because of its characteristic fear, anxiety, and insecurity, always worrying what other people think of us, whether they understand or appreciate us properly, and so on.

These kinds of thoughts that we harbor can come to rest through the practice of tranquillity meditation. So the torrential speed of the waterfall is now reduced to a meandering river. Our thoughts and emotions flow more easily now, and their impact is not so great as it was in the past. Thus we learn how to handle and express our thoughts and emotions, so that our meditation becomes a means of self-empowerment. We are no longer victims of our thoughts and feelings; in fact, we learn how to work with them. Like a gentle flowing river, we learn how to flow with our thoughts and emotions without being carried away by the current.

Finally, with shi-ne practice, the state of one-pointedness is attained, in which we realize that these thoughts and emotions arise from and disperse back into our natural state of being. This is like all the different rivers flowing back to a common destination—the ocean. We may have our own idiosyncratic, individualistic thoughts, emotions, and feelings, but they all have the same origin and they all disperse back into our own natural state of being. Hence the paranoid samsaric mind either ceases to operate or has no enduring influence.

In that way, as mentioned earlier, in Mahamudra meditation, one does not reject thoughts and feelings, but one becomes aware of them and relates to them. Also, knowing that the so-called mental defilements in fact have their origin in our natural state of being, knowing that they disperse back into the natural state of being, allows us to have confidence in ourselves so that negative thoughts and emotions have no power to disturb us. We have literally made peace with ourselves. This is how the yoga of one-pointedness is attained.

2. The yoga of nonconceptuality is not about just overcoming inhibitions and constrictions regarding our experiences in terms of emotions and feelings, but has to do with how we think, what we think, what we believe, and what we believe in. As it is said in the teachings, the experience of emotions and feelings lands us in our samsaric condition; that means we ourselves can find liberation from our self-imposed bondage. But we need to go further because in the context of Buddhism the practitioner learns how to overcome not only emotional afflictions, but also conceptual confusion, in order to obtain omniscience.

According to Buddhist teachings, including Mahamudra, as human beings (not as members of a particular race, religion, or culture), we subscribe to many misconceptions. For example, any human being from anywhere would have the idea that there is a self-existing, incontrovertible self; or may believe in political or religious ideas or systems as eternally, perennially true, detached from concrete, individual, social, environmental, political conditions. Now, according to these teachings, nothing we believe in or feel passionate about has any intrinsic reality.

On this level of the yoga of nonconceptuality, we are not asked to stop thinking or not to believe in anything; rather we must relinquish our fixations about what we believe in. In the West, we may believe in such things as feminism or democracy, but as Buddhists, although we may subscribe to ideas that we feel close to and have an affinity with, ultimately we should be nondogmatic about them. All issues or ideas are contingent upon external factors such as cultural, social, religious, or political climates of the times.

This is why the early Buddhist teachings themselves are referred to as a raft that we use to cross the ocean of samsara. The raft is important, but reaching the other shore is even more important. The yoga of nonconceptuality means that the practitioner learns how to rise above conflicting belief systems; while being able to subscribe to some and reject others, one even rises above those that one does subscribe to. As Buddhists we do believe in liberation or Buddhahood, yet even this belief system is something we learn to rise above.

3. The yoga of one taste is concerned with the realization of the coexistence of contingent worldly states of being and the liberated, untarnished, immaculate state of freedom and enlightenment. Having attained the state of one-pointedness and having realized nonconceptuality, the practitioner has to realize that he or she is still subject to conditioned existence. In other words, we still must work with the phenomenal world. We have to address social issues, personal issues, political issues, and spiritual development in a very concretely and manifestly material environment. We come to understand that the material world that surrounds and envelops us is not separate and distinct from the transcendental world of spirituality. Ultimate truth is present in everything that we come in contact with. It has to be stressed that what we realized in the yoga of nonconceptuality has not led us to ignore the world or dismiss our experiences of that world as insignificant. The empirical world and the transcendental world have the same nature because the ultimate truth is present in both, and in all of our experiences. That is, whether deluded or enlightened, there is just one flavor, one taste.

4. The yoga of nonmeditation (or the yoga of no more learning) refers to the enlightened state, and this yoga is self-explanatory. One is no longer on the path: the traveler has finally come home, reached his or her destination, and realized the ultimate truth. However, I would like to point out that attaining Buddhahood and understanding the ultimate nature of things does not mean the enlightened person does not need to formally learn anything, such as French or about the philosophy of Kant. To realize the nature of reality and to understand things on the empirical level of everyday life are quite different. Of course, these two worlds are not in opposition, as mentioned in connection with the yoga of one taste. However, it is evident that one who has attained the ultimate truth will not automatically be well versed in all fields of knowledge. Thus, "no more learning" simply means that there is nothing more to learn about the true nature of existence.

Finally, even though the Mahamudra tradition is being presented as being different from sutric Mahayana and tantric Mahayana, Takpo Tashi Namgyal, in the text *Moonbeam*, states clearly that the Mahamudra approach can be practiced independently of Tantra, without receiving tantric empowerment or even initiation. This is a distinctly unique practice to lead the practitioner to ultimate realization. It is true that one engages in tantric practice to realize Mahamudra; however, Mahamudra does not make use of deity practice, visualization, or recitation of mantras. The orientation of Mahamudra practices lies in trying to realize one's true nature. In that way Takpo Tashi Namgyal and others make it very clear that Mahamudra can be practiced and cultivated separately from tantric Mahayana.

At the same time, it has to be stressed that Mahamudra is often undertaken alongside sutric and tantric Mahayana practices. Takpo Tashi Namgyal also states that even though the Mahamudra system itself belongs to the so-called instantaneous approach to enlightenment, nonetheless, even within this system itself, it is gradual, and this is understood in relation to the four yogas of Mahamudra. The four-yoga system can be understood in relation to the five paths and the ten stages of the Bodhisattva, as described earlier. For example, the path of accumulation and the path of application of the sutric system correspond to the yoga of one-pointedness. The yoga of nonconceptuality corresponds to the path of insight. The yoga of one taste corresponds to the path of meditation in the sutric system. The yoga of nonmeditation corresponds to the ninth and tenth stages of the Bodhisattva, or the path of no more learning, which culminates in the eleventh bhumi or stage, which is equated to the attainment of Buddhahood.

To conclude, we can see the integrated nature of the whole spectrum of Buddhist philosophy and practice, even while there is variety and difference in terms of view and practice. I think it is very important to appreciate the underlying sense of unity and not think that one particular school of Buddhism, or one set of practices, is contradicting another. Tantric visualizations of deities are forms of normal meditation, which is made very clear in the Buddhist texts. Focusing on the visualization of deities is part of shamatha meditation; visualizing a deity as being translucent and not a substantial entity is an aspect of vipashyana meditation. What the Buddhist texts clearly indicate, but what some people fail to understand, is that it is important to see how one form of Buddhism has developed from another, instead of thinking that there were major revolutions taking place throughout its history.

Index

SHAMBHALA DRAGON EDITIONS

(continued on next page)

The Five Houses of Zen, translated by Thomas Cleary.

A Flash of Lightning in the Dark of Night: A Guide to the Bodhisattva's Way of Life, by Tenzin Gyatso, the Fourteenth Dalai Lama.

Glimpses of Abhidharma, by Chögyam Trungpa.

Great Eastern Sun: The Wisdom of Shambhala, by Chögyam Trungpa.

The Heart of Awareness: A Translation of the Ashtavakra Gita, by Thomas Byrom.

Kensho: The Heart of Zen, by Thomas Cleary.

Lieh-tzu: A Taoist Guide to Practical Living, by Eva Wong.

Living at the Source: Yoga Teachings of Vivekananda, by Swami Vivekananda.

Living with Kundalini: The Autobiography of Gopi Krishna, by Gopi Krishna.

Mastering the Art of War, by Zhuge Liang and Liu Ji. Translated and edited by Thomas Cleary.

The Mysticism of Sound and Music, by Hazrat Inayat Khan.

Nine-Headed Dragon River: Zen Journals 1969–1982, by Peter Matthiessen.

Returning to Silence: Zen Practice in Daily Life, by Dainin Katagiri. Foreword by Robert Thurman.

Rumi's World: The Life and Work of the Great Sufi Poet, by Annemarie Schimmel.

Shambhala: The Sacred Path of the Warrior, by Chögyam Trungpa.

The Shambhala Dictionary of Buddhism and Zen.

The Sutra of Hui-neng, Grand Master of Zen, translated by Thomas Cleary.

Vitality, Energy, Spirit: A Taoist Sourcebook, translated and edited by Thomas Cleary.

Wen-tzu: Understanding the Mysteries, by Lao-tzu. Translated by Thomas Cleary.

The Wheel of Life: The Autobiography of a Western Buddhist, by John Blofeld.

For a complete list, please visit www.shambhala.com.